What others are saying...

Discover!
America's Great River Road

"Having read *Discover!* I cannot now imagine traveling the areas without the maps, directions, narrative background and detailed information they contain. Bring your *Quimby's Cruising Guide*, but you must also have Pat Middleton to show you 'the rest of the story.'"

Review
HEARTLAND BOATING MAGAZINE

"This book is must reading! Pat Middleton has done super writing and research. The book is impossible to lay down for all the information it contains."

Orville Meyers, long-time host
of Iowa's radio and television program,
"Along the Outdoor Trails"

"A terrific guide for those who relish boating, fishing or cruising on land along the Mississippi River."

BOOKLIST MAGAZINE
American Library Association

"I drove the Great River Road from St. Paul to St. Louis last August, with this book at my side. When we passed out of its parameters, we felt a sense of loss. I eagerly await the release of further volumes." Review

ST. LOUIS POST DISPATCH

"The primary charm of *Discover!* lies in the author's down-to-earth fascination and interest in the towns and countryside of the Mississippi River." Hayward Allan

"Pat has done her homework very well."

Tom Klein, Publisher, Northword, Inc.

"The perfect guide for traveling the Mississippi River Valley. Travel tips and 'things to see and do' make this one of the best travel bargains around."

MIDWEST BOOK REVIEW

"Don't leave home without a copy of *Discover! America's Great River Road*. It will be a friend on the road, offering tips on things you won't want to miss as you travel down river." Review, DULUTH NEWS-TRIBUNE

*For information about Pat's other books, see page xv and **Ordering Information** on the last page of this book.*

Discover!
America's Great River Road
Volume 3, The Lower Mississippi

— ☼ —

ST. LOUIS, MISSOURI,
TO
MEMPHIS, TENNESSEE

by
Pat Middleton

Pat Middleton

Heritage Press • Wisconsin
Rt. 1, Stoddard, WI 54658
http://www.greatriver.com

Pat Middleton is also the author of
Discover! America's Great River Road, Volume 1
(St. Paul, Minnesota, to Dubuque, Iowa)
and *Volume 2* (Galena, Illinois to St. Louis, Missouri).

Cover Design by Heinecken Assoc. Ltd.
Chicago, Illinois

Visit the Mississippi River Home Page
http://www.greatriver.com

Contents

St. Louis & St. Charles, Missouri
A Brief History, Getting around Town,
St. Charles
INSIGHTS: Cahokia Mounds Historic Site; The Missouri River

Jefferson County, Missouri
Mastodon State Historic Site, Imperial, Kimmswick,
Herculaneum, Festus, Crystal City
INSIGHTS: The Ice Age; See the Gigantic Elephant Discovered
in These Regions!

St. Clair County, Illinois
Sauget, Cahokia, Dupo
INSIGHTS: Church of the Holy Family; Cahokia Courthouse
Historic Site; Chief Pontiac; Identifying Limestone Outcroppings;
Geologic Column

Monroe County, Illinois
Columbia, Waterloo, Maeystown, Fults
INSIGHTS: George Rogers Clark and His Long Knives; Sunflowers
in Illinois; Gloria (Maeys) Bundy, Monroe County Historian; Gene
Esker, Fisherman and Trapper

Ste. Genevieve County, Missouri
Ste. Genevieve
INSIGHT: The Flood of 1993

Preface

My husband and I are travelers. Over the course of five years, we lived in London, Bangkok, Sydney, and Aix-en-Provence, France. We snorkled over the Great Barrier Reef, photographed the sunrise on Ayers Rock, taxied up the Malay peninsula, sailed in Fiji. But it is the Mississippi River valley that called us home, partly because we have found here a little bit of everything we've admired most in the world.

The history of the river is significant not only to residents, but to the nation. Indian activity along the river dates back 10,000 years and more. European traders and explorers were active in the valley at the same time New York was a struggling village. Spain, France, England, and America have all made major investments in the discovery and exploitation of its adjoining shores.

Our recent visits to Tennessee and Kentucky delighted us, as they did during the spring breaks of my college days. Beginning in Missouri, we visited the campsite of Meriwether Lewis and William Clark. Then, in rapid succession, we marveled at the pyramid-high Cahokia Mounds, soared 630 feet to the top of the stainless-steel Gateway Arch, touched 300-year-old oak in the homes of Ste. Genevieve, re-acquainted ourselves with Elvis and his beloved blues in Memphis. We retraced the path of the Lower Mississippi in Mud Island, marveled at intricate quilts displayed in Paducah, searched out sandboils left by the earthquakes near New Madrid, and walked the scenic paths of the Shawnee Hills National Forest.

Something for everyone, we decided. Only the Great River, we found, was missing. Like Tom Sawyer, who shows up at his own funeral, it seems a ghost. This gateway to a wilderness, a natural highway for the westward expansion, molder of land and culture, the Great River today has either been veiled in levees that separate it from its villages or it has wandered away on its own. We speak of it, we protect ourselves from its careless meanders, we test ourselves against it, but we seldom see it.

Then, occasionally and without fanfare, it is *there*— visible from a high overlook or from the riverside park of a village that has not yet walled itself away from the river's fury. And it flows as grand, as brooding, as silent as we imagined it might.

I hope you find this guide useful and enlightening. I have visited cities, villages and waysides. I have met and share with you the stories of a diverse people. May it add to your enjoyment of the Lower Mississippi.

ACKNOWLEDGEMENTS

This volume, more than any other in the *Discover!* series, is not my own, but rather a reflection of what I have learned from those who live and work along the Great River. Tourism associations and historical societies in each of the towns along the river were eager to help. Maybe it is just "southern hospitality"; whatever it is, it extends beyond just doing a job to really trying to help.

As I visited, local associations arranged accommodations and guides who were not only knowledgeable, but who were themselves history buffs, river buffs, or published authors and experts in their fields.

My thank-you list must be long: Marion and Lynn Bock, Jim Perry, Ro Morris, Lenore Barkley, Sue Anckerman, Rob Beckerman and Vernon Meyer. Russ Graham, Bonnie Styles, and Jeff Saunders at the Illinois State Museum, Ray Smith from the Shawnee Hills National Forest, Sylvie Barker, Gloria Bundy, Andy West at Trail of Tears State Forest in Illinois, Darlene Spinks, and Mike Walton at Reelfoot Lake. Gene Esker, Will Flores, Steve Powell, Beau

Inman, Joe Bennett, Herb Meyer, Russ Garrison, Louise Ogg, Jerry Smith, Erik Reid, Molly McKenzie, Mark Westhoff, Dorothy Overson, and Ed Crow.

Bed & Breakfast operators often have a special interest in history, architecture or geology in a given area, so they are often asked to help host a visiting river buff. I've tried to list most of those with whom I stayed in the following chapters.

To Sue Knopf, my editor and designer, it was a relief to be able to turn the final "shape up" over to someone as capable and experienced as you are!

Finally to my patient family and friends, many thanks! It is hard to imagine that my little journey along the river has stretched into 10 whole years!!!

—Pat Middleton

Join the river buff community at
http://www.greatriver.com

The Lower Mississippi River Valley

How to Use This Book

THE ROUTE

The route suggested by the maps and commentary in this guide commences in St. Louis, Missouri, and proceeds to the restored historic towns of St. Charles (on the Missouri River) and Kimmswick (just south of St. Louis). Thereafter, the suggested route returns to Cahokia, Illinois, on the east bank of the river opposite St. Louis. From Cahokia to Memphis, Tennessee, the route follows the east bank south with periodic forays into Missouri.

Most of the route follows a series of state, national and county roads that have been officially designated as the "Great River Road." Occasionally the suggested route leaves the "official" roadway for what I call "side routes" that are closer to the river and historic and natural sites of special interest.

These areas of special interest include the French Colonial District in Illinois between Columbia and Kaskaskia, the Shawnee National Forest and Cache River Wetlands in southern Illinois, and "Swampeast" Missouri from New Madrid to Belmont. Each of these side routes is prone to frequent flooding, so common sense should be used during times of high water.

About the Great River Road

The state- and federally-designated Great River Road is signed with a green and white pilot's wheel. Established in 1939 with the cooperation of ten states adjoining the Mississippi River, the Great River Road Parkway is a program of federal, state, and county highway improvements along both sides of the river from Canada to the Gulf of Mexico. Scenic easements, roadside parks, scenic overlooks, off-road parks and forest, points of historical interest, and other public river-oriented facilitiesare abundant.

MAPS

Each chapter begins with a regional map showing the suggested route for that chapter as a heavy dotted line. City maps within chapters pinpoint specific attractions noted in the text.

SITE DESCRIPTIONS

Besides descriptions of historic towns and parks, this guide also offers local histories, natural history information, and listings of private amenities such as campgrounds, bed and breakfast inns (B & Bs), and seasonal/recreational attractions.

SYMBOLS

Special symbols identify different types of attractions throughout this guide:

↑■	Historic site	▰	Boat launch
A	Camping	▼	Wildlife sanctuary
�	Hiking	▲	Natural area
⊼	Picnicking	●●●	Suggested route

INSIGHTS

Each chapter contains one or more "Insights"—shaded boxes giving in-depth personal, historical or geological information. I hope you will enjoy the "up close and personal" interviews with people living along the river: the Assistant Curator at the Quilt Museum in Paducah, a commercial trapper and fisherman in Illinois, a descendent of the founder of Maeystown, Illinois, and more.

APPENDICES AND INDEX

The appendix includes several charts and timelines as well as tourism contacts for the traveler. A detailed index is also provided.

OTHER BOOKS IN THE DISCOVER! SERIES

Volume 1 of *Discover! America's Great River Road* begins in Prescott, Wisconsin, near St. Paul, Minnesota, and follows the Great River Road to Dubuque, Iowa. *Volume 2* guides the traveler from Dubuque and Galena, Illinois to Alton, Illinois, near St. Louis. Copies are available from many bookstores, libraries, and in gift shops along the river. See the last page of this volume for order information or visit our Web site:

http://www.greatriver.com/order.htm

A children's guide, **The Mississippi River Activity Guide for Kids,** is also available from Heritage Press in a teacher's edition or as a complete teacher resource kit.

HOW TO CONTACT THE AUTHOR

For even more heritage and natural history information, or to contact the author directly, visit the Mississippi River Home Page on the World Wide Web:

http://www.greatriver.com

St. Louis,
Missouri

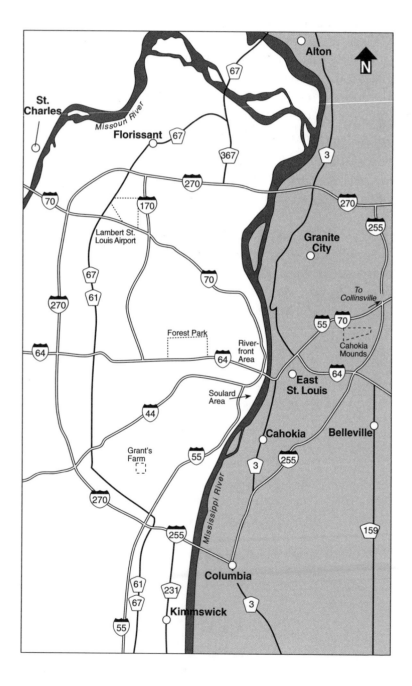

1

St. Louis & St. Charles, Missouri

City of St. Louis, Missouri

Population 380,000

For accommodation information and complete information on special events and what to see and do in St. Louis, contact the St. Louis Convention & Visitor Commission at 800-916-0040. A new Visitor Information Center is now open at the southeast corner of America's Center at 7th Street and Washington Avenue.

For many of us, the city of St. Louis is pretty well summed up by images of the soaring Gateway Arch and Christmas Clydesdales. The visitor will not be disappointed. Although it is one of the largest urban areas on the river, (the City of St. Louis is a separate entity from the County of St. Louis, which has a population of over one million residents in about 90 incorporated towns and cities) we found the main attractions and historic sites to be easy to find and well worth the journey. The city prides itself on an inordinate number of attractions and amusements that are available to children for $2 or less.

The main visitor attractions are conveniently bundled in a few separate areas: the **Riverfront**, the **Soulard Historic District**, and the **Forest Park** area.

The St. Louis Riverfront

The **Riverfront area** boasts riverboats, casinos, the **Jefferson National Expansion Memorial** and the **Gateway Arch.** Interstate 55 will take you right downtown, and we did not find parking or driving to be a problem. Just north of the Arch, within an easy walk of a block or two, is **Laclède's Landing.** Here old warehouses and other business buildings along the levee in the historic "old town" of St. Louis have been renovated into upscale shops and restaurants. Be sure to admire historic Eads Bridge—once hailed as the "impossible" bridge for its long span; its construction required massive investment and the development of new building technologies.

The **Metrolink** at Laclède's Landing comfortably carries passengers to **Forest Park, Union Station,** and **Busch Stadium.**

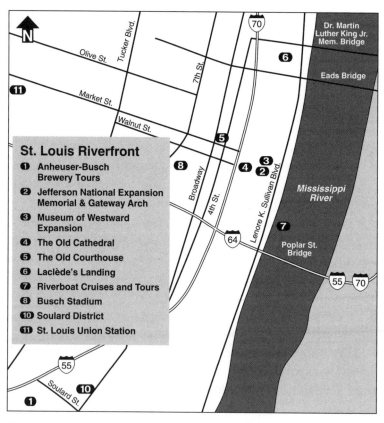

St. Louis Riverfront

❶ Anheuser-Busch
   Brewery Tours

❷ Jefferson National Expansion
   Memorial & Gateway Arch

❸ Museum of Westward
   Expansion

❹ The Old Cathedral

❺ The Old Courthouse

❻ Laclède's Landing

❼ Riverboat Cruises and Tours

❽ Busch Stadium

❿ Soulard District

⓫ St. Louis Union Station

Mississippi River

Dr. Martin Luther King Jr. Mem. Bridge

Eads Bridge

Poplar St. Bridge

Olive St.

Tucker Blvd.

7th St.

Market St.

Walnut St.

Broadway

4th St.

Lenore K. Sullivan Blvd.

Soulard St.

This light rail mass transit system is free within the inner city circle from 11 a.m. to 2 p.m. Monday through Friday. Or hop onto one of the little red and black **Shuttlebugs** that provide transportation the Forest Park Metrolink Station and the Park's attractions—Zoo, Science Center, Art Museum, and History Museum.

Lambert-St. Louis International Airport, 10701 Natural Bridge, (314-426-8000), one of the busiest airports in the world, is just 20 minutes away from the riverfront. Airport Express offers limo and taxi service to the airport.

WHAT TO SEE ON THE RIVERFRONT
Attractions listed alphabetically, keyed to Riverfront Map.

Anheuser-Busch Brewery Tours ❶

I-55 and Arsenal Street, 314-577-2626. Complimentary tours of the brewery include a visit to the Budweiser Clydesdale stables and hospitality room. Open Monday-Saturday, 9 a.m. to 4 p.m. Free.

While in St. Louis, we were thrilled to see huge trailers hauling the Budweiser Clydesdales—with the dalmation hanging his upper body out of the cab window!

Jefferson National Expansion Memorial & Gateway Arch ❷

Gateway Arch designed by Eero Saarinen, 314-425-4465. Small entrance and tram fees. Tram hours: 9:30 a.m. to 5:20 p.m. in winter; 8:30 a.m. to 9:20 p.m. in summer. The museum is open 9 a.m. to 6 p.m. in winter, 8 a.m. to 10 p.m. in summer.

630-foot high arch of stainless steel with a tram to viewing windows at the top. The soaring Arch, which commemorates St. Louis as the gateway to the west, can be seen from Alton, Illinois and Cahokia mounds on a clear day.

Museum of Westward Expansion ❸

Located below the Arch at the Jefferson National Expansion Memorial, 314-425-4465. Open daily from 8 a.m. to 10 p.m. in the summer, 9 a.m. to 6 p.m. in the winter.

A view from the Arch includes the Old Courthouse and Busch Stadium.

The Old Cathedral ❹

209 Walnut St. (231-3250). Open daily. This national landmark dates from the earliest days of St. Louis and is more than 150 years old. The first bishop of St. Louis is buried here.

The Old Courthouse ❺

11 N. 4th St., 314-425-4468. Open 8 a.m. to 4:30 p.m. Free.

Built between 1839 and 1862, the Courthouse contains historical displays of St. Louis and two restored courtrooms with displays explaining the Dred Scott trial. For more on Dred Scott, see Thebes Courthouse, page 125.

Laclède's Landing ❻

Just north of the arch and Eads Bridge. A stop on the Metrolink or an easy walk from the Arch and the President Casino on the Admiral. Upscale shopping, restaurants, special events.

This nine-block area of 19th century buildings and cobblestone streets is at the original site where Pierre Laclède, in 1764, set up his trading post after moving from New Orleans (via the Fort de Chartres area) with Mrs. Chouteau and their son, Auguste. Here was the center for fur trade on the Mississippi and Missouri Rivers; the gateway to the west. Brick buildings date from after 1849, when a huge fire burned steamboats and warehouses along the riverfront. Auguste Chouteau, at age 13, was given the responsibility of laying out Laclède's new community.

Riverboat Cruises and Tours ❼

Several paddleboats on the riverfront offer one-hour river cruises. 314-621-4040. On the riverfront, eat at the Lt. Robert E. Lee, *a permanently docked sternwheeler. 314-241-1282. The great cruising steamboats of the Delta Queen Steamboat Company may be docked near the steps of the Gateway Arch.*

Riverboat buffs will want to visit the **Golden Eagle River Museum,** 314-846-9073. It's located in Bee Tree Park in southern St. Louis County, 4.5 miles south of Interstate 270. Open 1 to 5 p.m., Wednesday through Sunday, May through October.

Riverboat Casinos

The President on the Admiral, 800-772-3647 (permanently moored).

Casino St. Charles, 800-325-7777 (permanently moored. Cruises on the Missouri.

Alton Belle Casino (Illinois), 800-336-7568.

Casino Queen (Illinois), 800-777-0777.

Riverport Casino Center, 800-599-6378 (permanently moored on the Missouri River in St. Louis County). Offers two Harrah's and two Players casinos.

International Bowling Hall of Fame and Museum and Cardinals Hall of Fame—Busch Stadium ❽

Located across the street from the Stadium, 314-231-6340. Open daily, 11 a.m. to 4 p.m. Stadium tours.

St. Louis baseball and bowling memorabilia including items relating to Stan Musial.

The Soulard Historic District

Just south of downtown, at the 7th St. exit off Interstate 55, this is one of the oldest and best known of the 79 distinct neighborhoods in the city. Here you'll find an open-air farm market, 19th-century homes, and outstanding live music and eateries. Contact the St. Louis Visitor Commission for a free guide to the ethnic neighborhoods of St. Louis.

Forest Park Area

Bounded by Kingshighway, Lindell and Skinker Boulevards.

Forest Park, at 1300 acres, is one of the largest public parks in the United States. In the late 1800s, it was still 1½ miles from the St. Louis city limits, and in 1904 it was the site of World's Fair. Today it provides space for three golf courses, picnicking sites, biking, skating, tennis and more. Several museums noted below are located on the park grounds.

WHAT TO SEE IN THE FOREST PARK AREA

Missouri History Museum (A)

At Lindell Boulevard and DeBaliviere Street in Forest Park, 314-746-4599. Open 9:30 a.m. to 5 p.m. Tuesday through Sunday, The city of St. Louis was named for Louis IX, the Crusader King , and a statue of him at the St. Louis Art Museum originally stood at the entrance of the 1904 World's Fair. Museum displays highlight the history of St. Louis and its river roots. The Lindbergh collection is here: his airplane, the *Spirit of St. Louis*; flight suit; passport; boots; flight plan and more. There is an excellent collection of regional books and historic photo reproductions for sale.

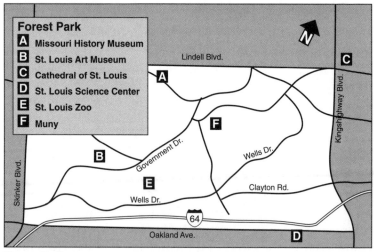

Forest Park area

St. Louis Art Museum (B)

Open Tuesday, 1:30 to 8:30 p.m.; Wednesday through Sunday, 10 a.m. to 5 p.m. Free.

Considered to be one of the finest art museums in the country, it is located in the **Fine Arts Palace**, which was the only building from the 1904 World's Fair meant to be permanent. The rest were made of plaster of paris and fiber and were meant to be temporary. A statue of Louis IX, the Crusader King, for whom St. Louis was named, stands in front of the Museum.

Cathedral of St. Louis (C)

4431 Lindell Blvd. and Newstead Avenue, 314-533-0544. Open daily, 9 a.m. to 5 p.m., May through September.; until 8 p.m. October through April. Must be seen for its interior mosaic art.

Exterior work began on this Romanesque-Byzantine style building in 1903 when it replaced the Old Cathedral at the riverfront. In 1946 the priest who had overseen the construction of the new cathedral was made a Cardinal. He became ill and died on the way back from his installation in Rome, never having walked in his church as a Cardinal. His red cardinal's hat still hangs from the ceiling inside the Cathedral. His hope was that when the cord rotted and the hat fell to the ground, it would serve as a reminder that all earthly power is temporal.

Ninety percent of the ceramic work in the church was done by a father and son team starting in the 1950s and continuing for 12 years, and then begun again in the '80s with the understanding that the son would carry on the ceramics work that his father had started.

St Louis Science Center (D)

5050 Oakland Ave, 314-289-4444. Free. Open Sunday through Thursday, 9:30 a.m. to 5 p.m.; Friday and Saturday, 9:30 a.m. to 9 p.m. Nominal fees for OMNIMAX Theater, planetarium, and Discovery Room.

Free exhibits include hands-on activities in aviation, technology, ecology, environment, and space. Life-size animated dinosaurs and more. St. Louis has been aptly described as "kid-friendly." The Science Center and the Zoo are perfect examples.

St. Louis Union Station ⑪

Market Street between Eighteenth and Twentieth streets. National Historic Landmark. (Hyatt Regency Hotel is upstairs).

This great train terminal was built in 1894 and modeled after Carcasson, the walled city of Charlemagne in France. It's filled with shops, restaurants, and boutiques under a grand vaulted ceiling of glass—renovated at a cost of $135 million.

St. Louis Zoo (E)

Forest Park, 781-0900. Open daily, 9 a.m. to 5 p.m.; until 8 p.m. on Tuesday in summer. Railroad, sea lion shows, movies, restaurants, gift shops. Free.

This world-class zoo (one of the top ten zoos in the country) is home to 3,500 animals in 83-acre park.

Muny (F)

This outdoor theater in Forest Park has 12,000 seats— 1500 free and the rest for sale in a range of prices. A seven-week series is offered from late June through mid-August.

St. Louis Area

Cahokia Mounds Historic Site and Interpretive Center

Collinsville, Illinois. Exit 24 off the I-255 to Collinsville Road, 618-346-5160—just minutes from downtown St. Louis. One of the largest pre-Columbian archeological sites in the world. See *Insight* on next page.

Grant's Farm

10501 Gravois, 314-843-1700. Open 9 a.m. to 5 p.m. from mid-April through mid-October. Free admission, but reservations required. Call first! Land originally owned by Ulysses S. Grant

INSIGHT

Cahokia Mounds Historic Site

As a **United Nations World Heritage Site**, Cahokia Mounds joins an elite group of cultural landmarks considered to be of international significance in the history of mankind. Others include the City of Rome, the Great Wall of China, the Pyramids of Egypt, the Taj Mahal in India, the Grand Canyon, Yellowstone Park, and the Florida Everglades.

Visitors can tour an area of 65 earthen mounds built by Mississippian Indians between 700 and 1400 AD and enjoy an outstanding multimillion-dollar interpretive center. The Mississippian Indian community here would have numbered between 20,000 and 40,000 individuals. Plan to spend an hour or more and be sure to see the 15 minute orientation slide show. A pamphlet with a suggested self-guided tour of the mounds is available.

Monk's Mound is the largest prehistoric earthen construction in the New World. It is larger even than the Pyramids of Egypt. From its summit, the Gateway Arch and the City of St. Louis are visible. The mound covers an area of 14 acres to a height of 140 feet. It is estimated that it would have taken 2000 men two years to haul enough clay to build the mound. In fact, it was built in stages over the course of 300 years.

The Mississippian population began a gradual decline about 1300, and by 1500, the city was abandoned. Whether this was a result of climatic changes, social problems, depletion of natural resources, or disease, is unknown. Later tribes inhabiting the area had no oral traditions or knowledge that might link them to the Mississippian culture.

Cahokia Mounds.

is now operated by Anheuser-Busch Co. Wildlife park, petting zoo, bird and elephant shows, Clydesdale barn.

National Shrine of Our Lady of the Snows

9500 W. Illinois, Hwy 15, Belleville, IL, 314-241-3400. Open 8 a.m. to 8 p.m. Free. Largest outdoor shrine in the world. Motel, gift shop, restaurant, eight devotional areas.

CAMPING IN THE ST. LOUIS AREA

Cahokia RV Parque, *4060 Mississippi Ave., Cahokia, IL 62206, 618-332-7700. Swimming Pool, showers, laundry. Exit 13 off 255 South.*

KOA Campgrounds, *South/Barnhart, 314-479-4449. Full hook-ups, store, pool, laundry.*

KOA Granite City, *3157 W. Chain of Rocks Road, Granite City, IL 62040, 618-931-5160. 80 campsites. All hookups, laundry, pool, camper, cabins, store*

St. Louis RV, *900 N. Jefferson, St. Louis, MO 63106, 314-241-3330 or 800-878-3330. A full-service RV park in downtown St. Louis. 24-hour security. Free bus service to downtown area.*

Yogi Bear's Jellystone Park Camp-Resort, *P.O. Box 626, Eureka, MO 63025, 314-938-5925. One-half mile to Six Flags Over Mid-America amusement park. Shaded sites, hookups, cabins, rental tents. Pool, mini-golf, store, laundry and much more.*

KOA Campgrounds West, *P.O. Box 128, Eureka, 63025, 314-257-3018. Full service campground. Cabins, Swimming pool, propane sales.*

St. Charles, Missouri
Population 60,000

Our first 24 hours in the St. Louis area were spent in historic Old St. Charles, nestled along the Missouri River 15 minutes west of the St. Louis International Airport. Follow I-70 west to the 5th Street exit.

I remember Old St. Charles for its limestone curbing, renovated warehouses, and everywhere the smell of river. Cobblestone seems to jut out most unexpectedly, so watch your feet!

A BRIEF HISTORY OF ST. CHARLES

Louis Blanchette, established *Les Petites Cotes* in 1769 as a trading post on the Missouri River. The Spanish renamed it St. Charles Borromeo in 1790. Neighboring Florissant was established 1786, Portage des Sioux to the north in 1779, Ste. Genevieve to the south as early as 1735, and St. Louis in 1764. Today, the "little hills" of St. Charles still cascade down to the riverfront.

Before the Europeans arrived, the Missouri, Osage, and Illinois Indians inhabited today's Missouri. The Illinois controlled the eastern third of the state, the Missouri the northwest, and the Osage the southwest. The Delaware and Shawnee, and then the Kickapoo, and Sacs and Fox, eventually displaced the Missouri and Osage, who were pushed further west by expanding American settlement.

In 1804, Meriwether Lewis and William Clark (the brother of George Rogers Clark) camped on the banks of the river in St. Charles

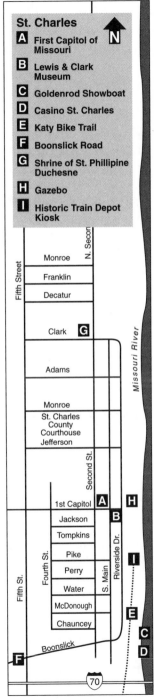

St. Charles

A First Capitol of Missouri

B Lewis & Clark Museum

C Goldenrod Showboat

D Casino St. Charles

E Katy Bike Trail

F Boonslick Road

G Shrine of St. Phillipine Duchesne

H Gazebo

I Historic Train Depot Kiosk

11

in preparation for their epic journey up the Missouri in 1804. Between 1821 and 1826, St. Charles served as the state capital for the new State of Missouri.

WHAT TO SEE IN ST. CHARLES

Look for the **Café Beignet,** one of many outdoor eateries in the Old Town. A *beignet* is a tasty fried French puff pastry sprinkled with powdered sugar—one can buy a can of beignet mix right at the café. Enjoy fine dining throughout the Old Town and Frenchtown districts.

First Capitol of Missouri (A) ⚑

200-216 S Main. 314-946-9282. Restored legislative chambers, interpretive center, and restored mercantile site from when St. Charles was the state capital from 1821 to 1826. Missouri State Historic Site. Tours Monday through Saturday, 10 a.m. to 4 p.m.; Sunday, 12 to 5 p.m. 10-minute video. Adjoining DNR Interpretive Center has books on the area.

Lewis & Clark Museum Historic Site (B) ⚑

701 Riverside Drive, 314-947-3199. 10:30 a.m. to 4:30 p.m.
Don't miss visiting this fascinating museum and trading

INSIGHT

The Missouri River

Father James Marquette noted when he saw the mouth of the Missouri emptying into the Mississippi River:

I have seen nothing more dreadful. An accumulation of large trees and branches, floating islands issuing from the Missouri (Pikitanoui) with such impetuosity that we could not without great danger risk passing through it.

During the summer of 1673, Marquette and Louis Joliet canoed the Mississippi River as far south as the mouth of the Arkansas River before they realized the Mississippi would reach the Gulf, not the Pacific. For statistics on the Missouri River, please see "Tributaries" on page 134.

---

post, located approximately where Lewis and Clark camped in St. Charles during the winter of 1804 preparing for an 8,000 mile expedition up the Missouri, to the Pacific, and back. Dioramas upstairs illustrate parts of the trip diary.

Documents show that the keelboat on display might have been loaded with trade goods: 4600 needles, 130 rolls of tobacco, 48 calico ruffled shirts, 2800 fishhooks, 132 knives, 72 pieces of striped silk ribbon, beads, 6 kegs of spirits (whiskey), 15 Harpers Ferry rifles, 24 tomahawks, 24 large knives, 6 lead containers of gun powder. A rare *metal trade beaver* on display was used by traders to represent one beaver pelt. One trade beaver purchased 1 pound of tobacco; 12 trade beavers bought one rifle. Trade beavers were widely used during the western rendezvous in the 1830s.

The renovated **Old Town Historic District** is just up the block from the Lewis & Clark Museum. More than 100 quaint shops and stores line the cobblestone streets. Live music and the sharp scent of barbecuing permeated the air the evening of our visit!!

Dinner Theater on the Goldenrod Showboat (C)

On the riverfront at Main Street, just north of the Blanchette Bridge. 1000 Riverside Drive, 314-946-2020.

Built in 1906, this National Landmark was considered to be the largest and finest showboat on the river in its time. The Broadway play *Showboat* (and Edna Ferber's novel of the same name) was inspired by this boat. Looking a little worn today, it is the only river showboat still on the river. It remains swathed in red velvet, and offers a popular dinner theater, box tables, and generally enjoys a full house. Dinner theater reservations are recommended.

Purchased in 1922 as **Menke's Showboat Legend,** the *Goldenrod* traveled through more than 15 states each year through most of the 1920s and '30s—more traveling than any other showboat in history. Many well-known performers have performed on its stage, including Jean Stapleton, Bob Hope, and Helen Hayes. Red Skelton got his start here when the boat was in St. Louis. He was an understudy and stage hand. When the main character broke his leg, Red had his chance.

Interested in learning more about showboats? Contact one of the following: *Showboat Centennial Newsletter,* 76 Glen Drive, Worthington, OH 43085; Philip Grahame's *Showboats, History of an American Institution.* University of Texas Press, Austin TX 78712; Billy Briant's *Children of Old Man River,* published by Lee Furmann, New York, NY.

Casino St. Charles (D)

Next door to the Goldenrod, *800-325-7777. Riverboat gambling.*

Katy Bike Trail (E)

For a map and information call Missouri DNR office at 800-334-6946. The Trail follows the old Missouri-Kansas-Texas Railroad bed along the Missouri River. Bike rentals are available in St. Charles. Eventually the trail will cover 200 miles.

The trail leads first to **Fort Defiance,** Daniel Boone's home for 20 years—314-987-2221 for information. **Augusta,** the beginning of Missouri's wine country, is about 30 miles away. For a Wine Country brochure, call 314-239-2715.

Boonslick Road (F)

A stone plaque in front of the big stone courthouse indicates that Boonslick Road goes from St. Charles to Franklin. It was a trace or pathway first marked by Indians, then trappers and hunters, and finally by Daniel Boone when he discovered the salt springs afterward called Booneslick. It was the main highway west, out of which grew the Salt Lake Trail, the Santa Fe Trail and the great Oregon Trail.

The Shrine of St. Philippine Duchesne (G)

619 N. Second St., 314-946-6127. Docent led tours are available Tuesday through Saturday, 9 a.m. to 11 a.m. and 1 p.m. to 3 p.m. Sunday tours are 1 p.m. to 3 p.m. only. Small suggested donation.

The Sacred Heart Academy and Mission is a huge stone boarding school, still active today, which commemorates its founder, Mother Rose Phillipine Duchesne (1769-1852). The shrine honors her early work with Native Americans as well as her elevation to sainthood in July of 1988. The Academy marks the beginning the historic **Frenchtown Antique District**. Frenchtown is actually older than the Old Town renovation, but it is not as well developed. There are numerous antique and specialty shops in the Antique District near Second and Third Streets.

ACCOMMODATIONS IN ST. CHARLES

St. Charles Visitor Bureau, 230 S. Main St., 63301, 800-366-2427.

Now on the internet at *www.historicstcharles.com*

Consider staying in a B&B right in one of the two historic districts, if possible—**Boone's Lick Trail Inn**, 1000 S. Main, 314-947-7000 or the **Elegant St. Charles House B&B**, 314-947-6221 in the heart of St. Charles. Other comfortable B&Bs include the **Lococo House**, 314-946-0619; **The Sage House**, 314-946-0619; and **Lady Bs**, 314-947-3421.

EVENTS & FESTIVALS

Third weekend in May: *Lewis & Clark Rendezvous* (Trader and military encampments, crafts, demonstrations, fife and drum corps parades.)

July 4th: *Riverfest*

Mid-August: *Fete des Petites Cotes* (19th Century Reenactment, Arts and Craft Displays.)

Labor Day weekend: *Ragtime Festival*

September: *Civil War Reenactment*

———————————— ⚓ ————————————

Leave St. Louis on I-55. Follow exit 186 east onto State Hwy. K, toward Kimmswick and Imperial, or west toward Mastodon State Historic Site.

Jefferson County, Missouri

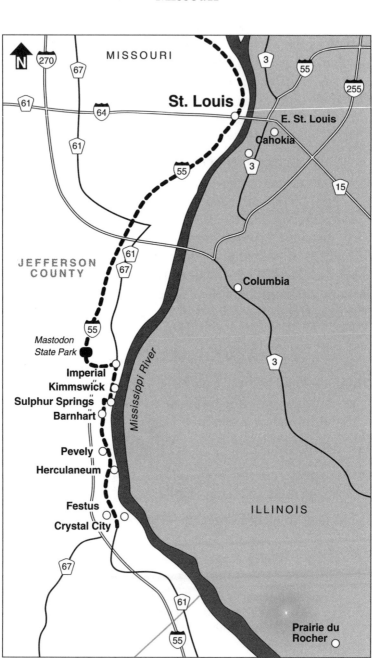

2

Jefferson County, Missouri

As you near exit 186 on Interstate 55, the modest sign announcing Mastodon State Historic Site suggests that this is one stop you can afford to miss. DO NOT PASS! A fascinating stop for kids and parents alike, this is the site of the Kimmswick Bone Beds and the historic discovery of Clovis spearheads intermingled with mastodon bones. The 425-acre Mastodon State Historic Site preserves this important archaeological site.

Mastodon State Historic Site

1551 Seckman Rd., Imperial, Missouri 63052, 314-464-2976.
Picnic area, hiking trails, and interpretive center.

The excellent interpretive center offers a large collection of fossilized bones, tusks, teeth and human artifacts from the site, as well as a full-size replica of a mastodon skeleton. Be sure to follow the short (¼-mile) trail to the bone bed. In spring, hillsides bloom with dogwood, redbud, and serviceberry. Mature forests of red, white, and chinquapin oak, shagbark hickory, hackberry, and eastern red cedar are a lush contrast to the flat cornfields just to the south.

The actual excavation area has been reburied for future study as new technologies develop. The last dig was in 1984, and it is conceivable that it will be 50 years before another one takes place here.

17

THE CLOVIS CONNECTION

Early American Indians referred to as Clovis hunters crossed paths with giant mastodons 11,000 to 12,000 years ago. Excavations at Kimmswick in 1979 by the Illinois State Museum Society produced the first and only complete Clovis projectile ever found in association with the bones and teeth of the American mastodon. This discovery at the Kimmswick Bone Beds was significant because it provided definitive evidence for the co-existence of the **American mastodon** and the **Clovis culture**.

The Clovis artifacts found at Kimmswick indicate that it was a site for killing and butchering of mastodons, and that chipped-stone weapons were manufactured at the site. The area was probably deciduous woodland and open grassy meadows with limited occupation by the Clovis hunters.

Clovis "points"

The Clovis people are considered to be the earliest successful group of Native Americans. They are believed to have arrived from northeast Asia at least 12,000 years ago via the Bering Straits, a 1300-mile-wide land bridge to North America. The Clovis people were nomadic, living in groups of about 50 men, women, and children. They were expert artisans and skilled big-game hunters, living side-by-side with mammoths, mastodons, camels, llamas, horses, peccaries, stag-moose, musk-oxen, saber-toothed cats, bears, lions, cheetahs, and dire wolves. The closest similar environment today would be the savanna of Africa. All the large animals associated with the Clovis culture became extinct by the end of the Ice Age.

In 1933, the first artifacts found with mammoth bones were discovered in Clovis, New Mexico. Since then, artifacts of the Clovis people dating from 11,300 to 10,900 years ago have been found from coast to coast. However, *Clovis/*

The Ice Age

The Pleistocene period, or Ice Age, stretched from 1.6 million to 10,000 years ago. Toward the end of that period, glaciers to the north were melting, sending streams of meltwater southward. Animals such as giant ground sloths, peccaries, and hairy, elephant-like mastodons roamed the grassy meadows and deciduous woodlands of the Mississippi River Valley. The area now contained in the Mastodon Historic Site was once a swampy area of mineral springs that became a graveyard for many of the large animals. The resulting Kimmswick Bone Bed has yielded bones from more than 60 mastodons and is considered one of the most extensive Pleistocene fossil beds in the United States.

Both mastodons and mammoths had trunks, tusks, and a large size. Mastodons were browsers, foraging among bushes and trees, often preferring spruce forests. They stood 8 to 9 feet at the shoulders and weighed around four tons. Mammoths were slightly larger and were adapted to grazing on the lush prairies. The Kimmswick site was probably an open deciduous forest environment unlike the spruce forest normally preferred by mastodons.

Fossil records indicate that there have been five families of elephant-like mammals (the *Proboscidea*), with as many as 100 different species, during the 40-million-year history of this order. Today only two species of two genera still survive—the African and Asian elephants. In 1979, it was estimated that there were 1.5 million elephants in Africa. Today, less than half that number survive. It is estimated that only 100,000 elephants will exist by 2005.

Mastodon model from Mastodon State Historic Site

INSIGHT

See the Gigantic Elephant Discovered in These Regions!

The mastodon bones near Kimmswick were discovered in May of 1839 and described as the *Missourium Kochii* or the *Missouri Leviathan*. Dr. Albert C. Koch, part scientist and part showman in the tradition of P. T. Barnum, supposed this mastodon was an entirely new species, different from the known mammoths and mastodon species at the time. He claimed that this mastodon was especially adapted to living for great lengths of time under water, similar to a hippopotamus, and envisioned the tusks sweeping back toward the animal's ears, as do the horns of a water buffalo. By 1840, he had amassed enough bones to mount a skeleton that he displayed in his St. Louis Museum (at a site almost directly beneath the present Gateway Arch) and throughout the United States and parts of Europe. The original Kimmswick mastodon bones were purchased by the British Museum in London.

An account in *Centennial*, a novel by James A. Michener, relates a visit by Levi and Elly Zendt to "see the Gigantic Elephant Discovered in These Regions by Dr. Albert Koch" when they passed through St. Louis on their way west in 1844. The Zendts, like most other immigrants in the western expansion, had never seen an animal so fearsome as the skeleton suggested.

From "Seeing the Elephant" by Jeffrey J. Saunders, Associate Curator of Geology, Illinois State Museum. The Living Museum, *Vol. 51, No. 3.*

mammoth remains occur only in Arizona, New Mexico, and from Texas and northward to South Dakota. Fewer than 15 Clovis sites nationwide, all on the western plains, are associated with mammoth bones. The *only* documented *Clovis/mastodon* site is at the Kimmswick Bone Beds.

ARMADILLOS IN MISSOURI?

Among other large animal bones found in rock beds and caves in the area of Mastodon State Historic Site are the remains of the extinct *Beautiful Armadillo.* This is of special interest to researchers in the Illinois and Missouri area as there are signs that the modern-day nine-banded armadillo may be expanding its range to include southern Illinois and Missouri. In 1993 the first confirmed Missouri spotting of an armadillo was made near Hillsboro, about 30 miles south of St. Louis. There have since been numerous sightings reported in the St. Louis area.

Scientists are studying with great interest the northerly expansion of the armadillo from the Rio Grande River Valley in southern Texas at the beginning of the 20th century. Is the modern-day armadillo invading new territory, or is it simply returning to an area previously inhabited by the species? While the *average* temperature of the Ice Age climate was much colder than it is today, the winters may not have been as extreme as they are now.

The Ice Age armadillo was identical to the modern-day armadillo except that it was two to three times larger. Its bones, teeth and bits of shell have been found in deposits that are over 10,000 years old. Scientists have found its fossils ranging throughout most of southwestern Iowa, central Missouri, and southern Indiana—almost identical to where modern-day armadillos have now been spotted.

Should you see an armadillo in Missouri or Illinois, please report your observation to the Research and Collections Center, Illinois State Museum, 1920 S. 10½ Street South, Springfield, IL 62703, or call 217-785-4844. You will add to researchers' understanding of why, how, and when armadillos expand or contract their ranges.

Imperial, Missouri

Imperial, once known as West Kimmswick, is a small village just off the highway on the way to Kimmswick. A local attraction features a retired cougar and the woman who appeared with it in the Mercury television commercials.

Kimmswick, Missouri
Population 160

Located 20 miles south of St. Louis and just east of the Kimmswick Bone Beds, the little village of Kimmswick was founded in 1859 by German immigrant Theodore Kimm. (The word "wick" in German means "town.") It is one of a handful of picturesque restored villages now found along the length of the Mississippi River. While it was a popular pleasure stop during the steamboat days, the highway system bypassed it, bringing an abrupt and early end to growth and development.

The restoration of Kimmswick is due largely to a small group of visionaries, led by Lucianna Ross, who saw commercial development as a way to preserve the deteriorating 1800s-era village. The first restoration effort began with the Kimmswick General Store. Today nearly thirty historic buildings have been preserved as craft shops, bed & breakfasts, restaurants, antique and gift shops. The shops are closed on Mondays and open from 11 a.m. to 5 p.m. on all other days.

The Burgess-How House was the first log cabin to be resettled and restored in Kimmswick; there are now several more, mostly clustered in the block bounded by 2nd, Elm, 3rd and Oak Streets. None of the log cabins in town were originally located in Kimmswick. Forty-four historic sites are listed in a Walking Tour Guide available at the museum, and four homes are open for tours.

WHAT TO SEE IN KIMMSWICK

El Camino Real Marker (A)

As you enter Kimmswick via Highway K, there is an historic marker at the bridge crossing Rock Creek, near

Highway 61-67. A granite boulder marks the 1789 Indian trail that officially linked St. Louis with settlements south along the river as far as New Madrid. After 1850, it became known as Telegraph Road, since the establishment of the first telegraph line west of the Mississippi was along this route.

The Burgess-How House and Museum (B)

3rd & Elm Streets. Open Tuesdays and Sundays.

This building serves as the Kimmswick Museum and is furnished with primitive antiques to resemble a home in 1840. A photo record of early Kimmswick and historic river floods is displayed in the museum.

Barbagallo House (C)

A small log cabin (the Winery, c. 1859), sits next to the three-story French-style Barbagallo House (c. 1850) at the corner of 2nd and Oak St. Note the gallerie porch and orig-

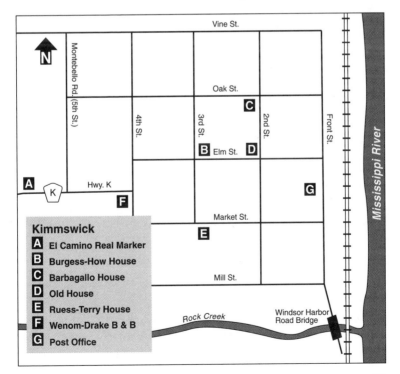

Kimmswick
- **A** El Camino Real Marker
- **B** Burgess-How House
- **C** Barbagallo House
- **D** Old House
- **E** Ruess-Terry House
- **F** Wenom-Drake B & B
- **G** Post Office

Barbagallo House

inal rain gutters of the Barbagallo House. A mill wheel out front still contains grooves for grinding grain. The stone wheels without grooves (the runner stones) were weights which lay on top of the grooved wheel.

The Old House (D)

2nd and Elm Streets.

Built around 1770, this is the oldest building in Kimmswick. It originally stood in the Arnold area where, in its early days, it served as a stagecoach stop. General Ulysses S. Grant is said to have frequented the Old House often. Today it again serves as an eatery.

Ruess-Terry House (E)

3rd and Market Streets.

Market Street is the main street in town. The Ruess-Terry House (c. 1866) is the oldest original building in Kimmswick, built by a German immigrant and miller, Peter Bruhn, of handmade bricks. Look for fish-scale shingles, a German architectural touch, on the gables of older homes in Kimmswick.

WHERE TO STAY AND DINE IN KIMMSWICK

There are two comfortable bed & breakfasts in town: **Wenom-Drake B&B (F)** and **Kimmswick Corners**. Eat at the

Commercial development of historic homes and buildings allows the restoration and preservation of old Kimmswick.

Blue Owl, 2nd and Mill Streets. The **Post Office** at Front and Market Streets **(G)** still hand-cancels stamps. For group tours or further information on special events and lodging, contact the Kimmswick Historical Society, Box 41, Kimmswick, Missouri 63053, 314-464-TOUR.

ANNUAL EVENTS IN KIMMSWICK

October, last full weekend: *Apple Butter Festival.* Nearly 20,000 visitors pour into tiny Kimmswick for this festival of historic arts and crafts. Park at Windsor School and ride the shuttle bus into town. Enjoy homemade apple butter made with Jonathan and Golden Delicious apples from Grafton, Illinois. Furniture, food, and craft booths are open from 11 a.m. to 5 p.m. daily.

December, first full weekend: *Candlelight Tour.* Historic homes are decorated in holiday themes for public touring. 5 p.m. on Friday and Saturday, 3 p.m. on Sunday.

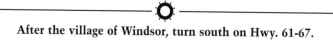

Follow Front Street out of town to Windsor Harbor Road for
a pleasant rural drive to Hwy. 61 and south through the
towns of Windsor, Sulphur Springs, Barnhart,
Herculaneum, Festus and Crystal City.

The bridge crossing Rock Creek, just at the south edge
of Kimmswick, originally spanned the River Des Peres in
St. Louis county and is now on the National Historic Register. It was built by the Keystone Bridge Co. in 1874, the
same year the Eads Bridge was built in St. Louis.

All three bridges in this area were under water during
the flood of 1993. The bright yellow **Grimshaw home** near
the 1874 Windsor Harbor Road Bridge had water up to its
lower windows. The big white house overlooking the creek
was a riverboat captain's house.

The white, riverside **Anheuser Home**, originally called
Fred-Mar Farm, was built by a relative of the St. Louis
brewery family. Next door, visit **Hoppies Harbor** for a
scenic river view. This is a public marina and river access.
Note the river gauge on top of the riverbank—well above
normal river levels.

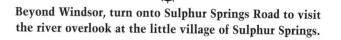

After the village of Windsor, turn south on Hwy. 61-67.

This stretch of highway was covered by about 5 feet of
water during the floods of 1995. The apparently dry and
harmless creekbeds beside the highway become life-threat-
ening in flash flood situations.

Beyond Windsor, turn onto Sulphur Springs Road to visit
the river overlook at the little village of Sulphur Springs.

An old rock wall and watchtower along Highway 61 once
surrounded the property of a very wealthy family. The low
rock walls around many of the homes in Sulphur Springs

Hoppies Harbor. Note the high water marker by the tree.

are intended to protect homes from floodwaters! There is no access to the town during major floods—which may last as long as three months, as they did in 1993 and 1995. The high riverside overlook presents a beautiful stretch of open river. Many of the homes here date from about the 1870s.

WHERE TO CAMP IN THE BARNHART AREA

KOA Camping ▲

Exit 185, just south of Barnhart at 8000 Metropolitan Blvd., 314-479-4449. There is a second KOA campground at Jefferson Resort, Hwy. 67, 314-586-7448.

Pevely is home to Foster Glass, Dow Chemical, Carondolet Corporation and the I-55 Race Track. There is a huge flea market on Saturdays and Sundays along Old State Road. Pevely is not on the river and does not offer any notable amenities or attractions for the traveler.

The big stone house on the west side of the road just before Herculaneum is known as the **Landmark Building**. It was built in 1863 and long served as a stagecoach stop or inn. Its walls are 24 inches thick.

Herculaneum, Missouri
Population 350

Founded in 1808, Herculaneum is one of the older permanent settlements below St. Louis. According to legend, it is the site of the first Protestant sermon west of the Mississippi River. Its first post office was established in 1811, and it became the Jefferson County seat in 1819. St. Joseph Lead Co. constructed a lead smelter here in 1890.

WHAT TO SEE IN HERCULANEUM

Dunklin and Fletcher Memorial Park

Public picnic ground with a trail along the side of the bluff in the northeast corner of the picnic ground.

This park offers an excellent overlook of the river, though tree growth is starting to obscure the view. One of the first lead shot towers west of the Mississippi River was established on the riverbank below the park in 1809. The old shot tower is visible off to the right as you face the river.

The park is named after Thomas Fletcher (1827-1899), the first native-born governor of Missouri, who served from 1865 to 1869, and Daniel Dunklin, who served as the fifth Missouri governor from 1832 to 1836.

Festus, Missouri
Population 8105

Limestone mined from the white bluffs in this area is of high quality, used mostly for paving and cement. Behind the first mall on the west as you drive south, there are big holes in the bluff face—openings from silica sand mines. During the war, ammunition was stored in the cool mine caverns.

Crystal City, Missouri
Population 4088

Turn off Highway 61 onto 11th Street in Crystal City. Drive past a park and a cemetery, toward the river to **Huss Landing**. An Ursuline convent is located nearby. The French Ursuline Sisters arrived in "New France" in 1727 and maintained convents in both old French Canada and along the Lower Mississippi River. The oldest building on the Mississippi is an Ursuline convent built in 1744 and located in New Orleans.

Crystal City was named for the high-quality local silica sand which is used in the production of glass. The old Pittsburg Plate Glass Co. office has been renovated into the **Crystal City Museum** at the corner of Bailey and Mississippi Streets. The museum is closed on Mondays. Pittsburgh Plate Glass was known throughout the world for the manufacture of windshields, soda bottles, baking dishes, and other glass products.

---- ☼ ----

Continue south on I-55 or Hwy. 61 to Ste. Genevieve, p. 61,
or
Return to St. Louis and cross the river to tour the French Illinois Colonial District between Cahokia, Illinois and Prairie du Rocher, p. 31.

St. Clair County, Illinois

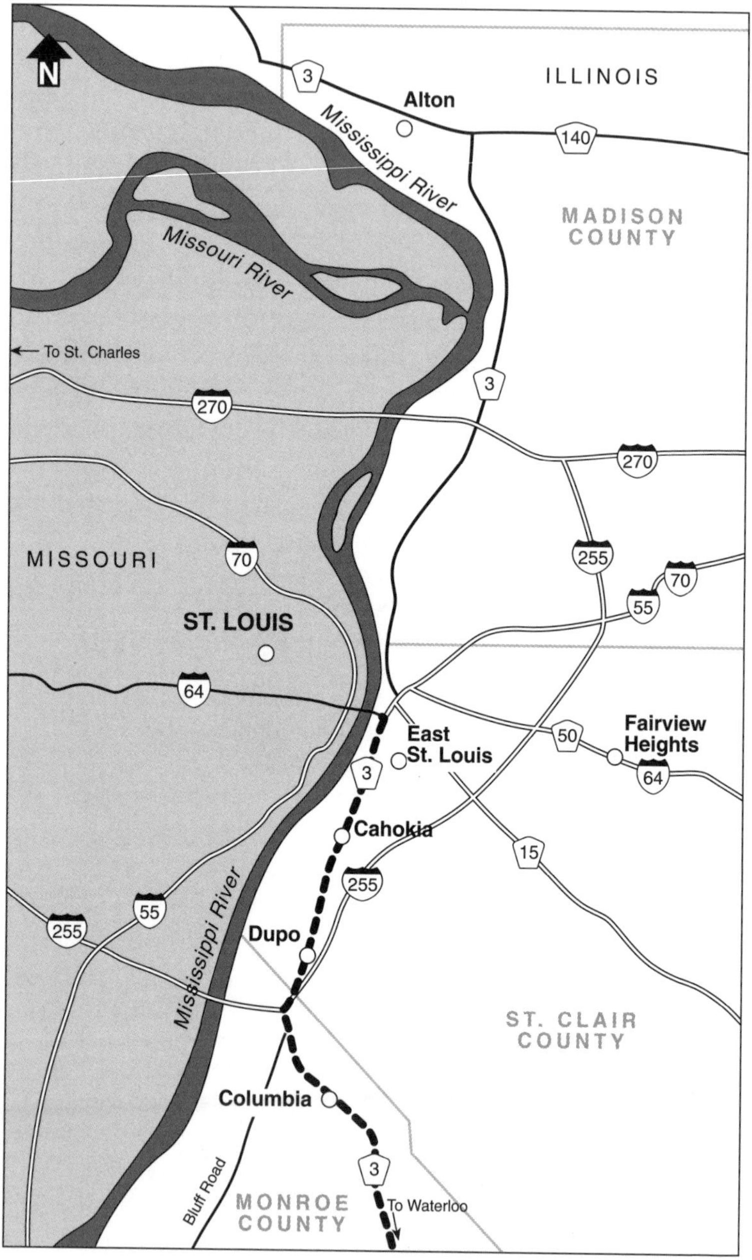

3

St. Clair County, Illinois

The urban sprawl surrounding the historic city of St. Louis spills over onto the Illinois shore, providing a fast-paced contrast to the rural communities that dot most of the Great River Road and the Mississippi River. The travel tip of the day is: *Avoid leaving or entering St. Louis during rush hours.* From Alton, Illinois, north of East St. Louis, to Waterloo, south of Cahokia, the crush of commuters, malls and fast food restaurants has swallowed up many historic sites in communities that started as some of the first American settlements on the Mississippi.

Immediately south of Cahokia, the immensely fertile, flat "American Bottom" stretches south to the mouth of the Kaskaskia River. The American Bottom covers more than 400 square miles (288,000 acres), most of which is in Randolph, St. Clair, Monroe, and Madison counties. The table-flat fields are comprised of alluvial deposits—the silt-filled channel of an ancient river that carried meltwater

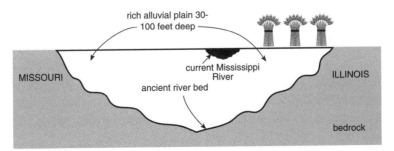

from ice sheets to the north. Silt fills the old channel to a depth of more than 100 feet in some places. Today only the small channel of the present Mississippi River remains to wander over the alluvial plains.

South of Cahokia, limestone bluffs rim the eastern edge of the flatlands for nearly 50 miles, from Dupo to just south of Modoc in Randolph County. Bluff Road, at the edge of the bluffs, is our route through most of Monroe and Randolph counties.

Bluff Road hugs the bluffs bordering the American Bottom.

HISTORY OF ST. CLAIR COUNTY

St. Clair County was named for Arthur St. Clair, a native Scotsman who acted as President of the Continental Congress and the first governor of the Northwest Territory in 1788. He was a well-known Revolutionary War veteran, associated with George Washington. Upon retirement, he returned to his farms in Bedford County, Pennsylvania.

During the 1700s, French settlements in the American Bottom supplied virtually all the wheat, grain, and much of the meat and salt for every French and Canadian colony in the New World. Goods were shipped south to New Orleans, and then north to Quebec via the sea and the St. Lawrence River.

Sauget, Illinois

The Big River Zinc Corporation and a petrochemical plant of Monsanto Chemicals operate along Illinois Highway 3 between Sauget and Cahokia, just south of East St. Louis. The Monsanto plant manufactures chemical intermediates for sale to other manufacturers. Many of the elements that go into STP gas additives are produced here in bulk. Monsanto's world headquarters are in St. Louis.

Casino Queen

The Casino Queen is moored at 200 S. Front Street, East St. Louis, IL 62201. Follow Highway 40 or 70 to the 4th Street Exit in East St. Louis and follow the signs. 800-993-ARCH.

☼

Follow Illinois Hwy. 3 south to Cahokia.

Cahokia, Illinois
Population 19,000

I did not expect to find the 200-year-old Church of the Holy Family standing, slightly skewed, in the middle of a 1950s suburban housing development in Cahokia. But this is a community that numbered only twelve residents (French-Canadians) in 1723 and then ballooned from 500 residents in 1950 to 20,000 in 1960! Visitors will find hotels, RV parks, and a city park just off Route 3. The main shopping area and subdivisions are stretched out along Route 157 to the east.

HISTORY OF CAHOKIA

Cahokia, which began as a French Canadian mission settlement 300 years ago, was the first permanent European settlement in what is now Illinois. In 1698, a mission party guided by Henri de Tonti established this site as an outreach to 2000 Tamaroa and Cahokian Indians living in the area. The Mission of the Holy Family, established in 1699 by Father St. Cosme from the French Seminary of Foreign

33

Missions in Quebec, soon attracted a small community of French Canadian traders and farmers.

In 1790, Cahokia became the seat of St. Clair County, a huge territory which included nearly eighty of the northernmost counties of modern Illinois. Constant flooding of Cahokia by the Mississippi and the growth of St. Louis and East St. Louis soon robbed Cahokia of its influence, and the county seat was moved to Belleville in 1814.

WHAT TO SEE IN CAHOKIA

Church of the Holy Family

Open during summer hours (June, July, August), 9 to 4 Monday through Friday, 618-337-4548. For more information, see next page.

Nicholas Jarrot House

Next door to the church is the Nicholas Jarrot House, built in 1810. Visible only from the outside, it is not normally open to the public. Jarrot fled the French revolution with a group of priests and arrived in Cahokia about 1794 via New Orleans. He prospered as a merchant, trader, and land speculator. His home, the oldest brick building in the State of Illinois, remains remarkably intact.

Church of the Holy Family, Cahokia

Church of the Holy Family

The distinctive vertical logs and white mortaring typical of French Colonial architecture make it easy to find this National Historic Landmark on the east side of Highway 3 almost immediately at the northern city limits of Cahokia.

The current church building was dedicated in 1799 as a church of the Diocese of Baltimore, which then comprised all of the original territories of the United States. Today it is part of the Diocese of Belleville and is the oldest church west of the Allegheny Mountains.

I arrived at the church shortly after a funeral had been conducted and found myself standing alone in the open sanctuary, sensing that this was the completion of a pilgrimage. This church is one of four major historic sites that stand witness to the Colonial French who tamed this swampy wilderness. The others are the historic homes in Ste. Genevieve, Missouri, the Pierre Menard Home, and Fort de Chartres in the Illinois bottoms.

In the room is a very real sense that the congregational prayers poured out over 300 years still breathe inside the simple, dim interior.

Axe marks stand sharp in the hand-hewn black walnut logs which would have been plastered over and whitewashed by the French-Canadian congregation. The smoothly polished floor betrays its hand-hewn nature by a subtle waviness. On a side table toward the front of the church is a chalice carried down the river by canoe from Quebec. A monstrance (a holy vessel) is stamped *Fabriqué en Paris, 1717*. An open family Bible is dated 1568. Flags of Britain, France and Colonial America hang above the entry.

Outside, a marker commemorates settlers buried here: Saucier, Touchée, Trottier, Poupard, Pelletier, Gagne, Du Charme, Beaulieu, and Dubuque. As modern construction unearths their bones, they are reburied in the vault at the base of the crucifix in the yard behind the church. Their names are still common in Cahokia today.

Cahokia Courthouse State Historic Site & Museum ⊤■

107 Elm Street, Cahokia, IL 62206, 618-332-1782. Open year round, Tuesday through Saturday from 9-5 p.m. For more information, see next page.

Martin/Boismenue House ⊤■

One mile south of Cahokia on old Illinois Route 3 in Prairie du Pont (commonly called Dupo, short for "du Pont").

A third major French historic site near Cahokia, the Martin/Boismenue House is listed on the National Register of Historic Places. It is at once the most recent Illinois restoration and the oldest known residence in Illinois. Recently dated to about 1790, its vertical log, post-on-sill construction has been exquisitely restored inside and out. Nearly 80 percent of the original structure remains intact. Most of the restorations have been hand crafted by skilled artisans. Its original occupant, Pierre Martin, was a second or third generation immigrant from Quebec. A middle-class land speculator, Martin eventually was forced to sell the home to repay debts.

CAHOKIA AREA SPECIAL EVENTS

April: *Annual Belleville Art & Craft Spring Festival,* Belleville, IL. Belle-Clair Expo Building, Rt. 159 & 13, 618-233-0052.

April: *American Indian Celebration,* Belleville, IL. National Shrine of Our Lady of the Snows, 618-397-6700.

August: *Midwest Salute to the Masters Art Festival,* Fair View Hts., 800-442-1488.

Shrove Tuesday: *Fête du Bon Vieux Temps,* Cahokia. Colonial Mardi Gras Celebration, 618-332-1782.

———————————☼———————————

Continue south toward Dupo and Columbia on Route 3 and I-255, the national route of the Great River Road.

Cahokia Courthouse State Historic Site and Museum

The old courthouse sits behind the modern city hall on the commons of the colonial village. Built sometime between 1735 and 1760, it is an excellent example of *poteaux-sur-solle* (post-on-sill) construction. The black walnut logs stand upright on a horizontal sill-log which rests on the original two-foot-thick stone foundation.

The excellent museum of Colonial French and American history inside the courthouse explains much about everyday life in the early settlements. The Indian trade, slavery, and colonial government left a legacy that affected Illinois history to the present day.

A model house inside shows both the upright log and cantilevered roof style of construction so common among the French. The wide spaces between the logs (*interstices*) were filled with stones and mortar (*pierrotage*). The courthouse was finished throughout in walnut, elm and white oak on oak beams, accounting for its great durability. Note the wrought iron candle chandelier in the main courtroom. The chandelier was lowered by rope and pulley to light the candles.

Though the Cahokia Courthouse is a fine looking building today (below), it is many times restored. It was moved and reconstructed twice, first at the World's Fair in St. Louis in 1904 and then in Chicago. It was finally returned to Cahokia, where restoration commenced in 1939 after its original foundations were discovered by archeologists. Flood damage and trees had certainly taken their toll (left).

INSIGHT

Chief Pontiac, 1720-1769

Pontiac, an Ottawa Indian, is most remembered from portraits that show him covered from head to toe with tattoos. A solid French sympathizer, he reputedly had either a *fleur-de-lis* or a sun for the Sun King, Louis XIV, on his chest. His main accomplishment was organizing the Indians to fight the English on behalf of the French during the French and Indian War.

In May of 1763, his anti-British confederacy posed simultaneous, surprise attacks on all British posts west of the Appalachians. All but three British forts were taken, resulting in the deaths of 2,000 unprotected British settlers. Pontiac himself led the unsuccessful attack on Detroit. The result was a new, more lenient British Indian policy.

During his last years, he lived in the city of St. Louis. He was bludgeoned to death after visiting friends on the site of the present-day Chief Pontiac Trailer Court, at the corner of Second Street across from the Courthouse Visitor Center.

The History of Illinois from 1884 tells the story of his death this way:

> *There was an English trader in the village at the time, who approached a vagabond Indian of the Kaskaskia tribe, and bribed him with a barrel of whiskey to execute Pontiac. The Kaskaskian followed Pontiac into the woods and buried a tomahawk in his brain. Pontiac's allies flew to neighboring nations to spread the story of Pontiac's death. Swarms of Sacs, Foxes, Potawatamies and other northern tribes, who had been fired by the eloquence of the martyred chief, descended to the plains of Illinois, and whole villages of Illini Indians were extirpated. A friend and ally from the French and Indian War was stationed at Fort de Chartres. He buried Pontiac's body nearby.*

Dupo

The tailings from the Dupo limestone mines are clearly visible just south of Cahokia. While mining occurs along the bluff throughout this area, it is only here that surface mining is devouring the bluffs. More often there will be large, gaping holes in the bluff face where limestone or sometimes silica sand is being mined. On a hot day, the 54 degree air flowing from the mines can be felt on the road.

At the junction of Sand Bank Road and Illinois Highway 3, one must choose whether to follow the official Great River Road along Highway 3 or turn off on Sand Bank Road to follow Bluff Road, which runs along the base of the bluffs, toward Prairie du Rocher. This is literally a choice between the high road and the low road. Frequent flooding makes the "low" road too unreliable to be officially designated as part of the Great River Road.

This guide suggests a little bit of both, following Highway 3 up onto the upland plains through Columbia and Waterloo.

---- ☼ ----

At Waterloo, follow Hwy. 156 and Maeystown Road to Maeystown. From Maeystown, wind back down to the bottom of the bluffs and follow Bluff Road to Modoc.

INSIGHT

Identifying Illinois Limestone Outcroppings

The limestone bedrock clearly visible along Bluff Road from Columbia to Prairie du Rocher may be identified as follows, oldest to youngest. Source: *Arrowheads to Aerojets, Monroe County, Illinois, 1673-1966*, edited by Helen R. Kline, published by Myron Roever Assoc.

Kimmswick Limestone is a very pure, light colored crystalline limestone with very little *chert*. (Chert is a very hard rock packed with minute quartz crystals, often substituted for flint by the Native Americans.) Kimmswick limestone is found at the Columbia Quarry at Valmeyer. Because of its purity, it is often used for chemical purposes.

Fernvale Limestone is a very thin layer, usually less than two feet. It is an impure, cherty brown limestone lying directly on top of the Kimmswick layer.

Maquoketa Shale is a fine, olive green shale which forms slopes rather than cliffs (low resistance to erosion). Locally, it may grade into a granular shaley dolomite.

Mississippian Era Limestones (noted below) were laid down about 400 million years ago when the Midwest lay at the equator and was covered by a shallow sea. Mud and sand carried into the sea by streams were deposited on the sea floor in layers. In time, they hardened into sedimentary rocks, the mud becoming shale and the sand forming sandstone.

Limestone was formed mostly from shells, corals, and other sealife as shells and skeletons were cemented together. Most fossils are found in the limestones and shales. Look for them at road cuts, old quarries and mines or along stream beds. Fossils in this area are exclusively marine organisms.

Fern Glen Formation is a limestone with chert bands. It is a deep red color and lies directly on the vastly older Maquoketa Shale (of Ordovician Age).

There are two "lost" intervals of rock in the order above. The fact that the entire Silurian and Devonian periods are missing indicates that the missing layers were deposited, but eroded away before the transgression of the Mississippian seas.

Burlington Limestone is a thick chert band with streaks of white limestone that comprises only 20-50% of the rock.

St. Louis Limestone is high in the geologic column. It underlies a much larger area than any other type of limestone. It is light colored, gray, bluish gray, or nearly white, dense, and fine textured.

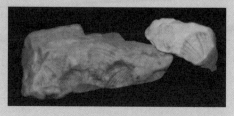

The Brachiopods, sometimes called "lamp shells" are the most common fossils in many areas.

INSIGHT

Geologic Column

SYSTEM Group, Stage	Formation	Thick- ness	Description
QUATERNARY			Loess
PENNSYLVANIAN		65	Sandstone, siltstone, shale, limestone, coal
MISSISSIPPIAN	Ste. Genevieve	70	Limestone, oolitic, chert
	St. Louis	245	Limestone, some dolomite some chert
	Other Mississippian	230	Limestone, chert, some shale
	Burlington	100	Limestone, very cherty
	Fern Glen	60	Limestone, some chert, shale
DEVONIAN			Shale
SILURIAN			Dolomite, cherty
ORDOVICIAN Maquoketa		150	Siltstone, shale, some limestone
Kimmswick		150	Limestone
OLDER ORDOVICIAN & CAMBRIAN		2450	Limestone, dolomite
PRECAMBRIAN			Granite, other igneous and metamorphic rocks

Monroe County,
Illinois

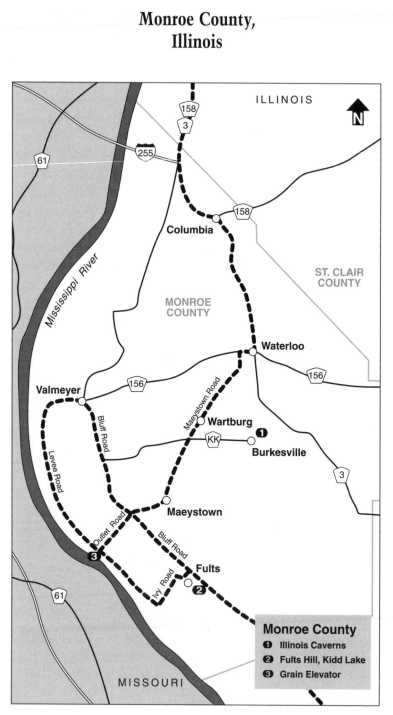

ILLINOIS

MONROE COUNTY

ST. CLAIR COUNTY

MONROE COUNTY

Mississippi River

Columbia

Waterloo

Valmeyer

Wartburg

Burkesville

Maeystown

Fults

MISSOURI

Bluff Road

Levee Road

Outlet Road

Maeystown Road

Ivy Road

Monroe County
❶ Illinois Caverns
❷ Fults Hill, Kidd Lake
❸ Grain Elevator

4

Monroe County, Illinois

French, American and German settlements lend an historic interest to a county that is otherwise intensely agricultural. Corn, soybeans, wheat and milo (an animal feed that's almost as profitable as corn) grow in the rich loess soil covering the upland plains and the fertile alluvial deposits of the American Bottom, a 90-mile crescent of exceptionally fertile floodplain stretching from roughly Alton, Illinois to just below Kaskaskia. Agriculture has made Monroe County one of the wealthiest counties per capita in the United States—a fact that is apparent from all the banks in Waterloo, the county seat!

Wheat is planted in the fall and harvested in June. Immediately after the wheat harvest, corn and soybeans are planted for fall harvests. The soybean crop is shipped via barge to New Orleans, where much of it goes on to Russia. In the fields, streams of golden corn pour directly from harvesters into trucks, which then rumble along Levee Road to Outlet Road and the elevator where grain is loaded onto the barges.

The topography of Monroe County is described as *karst*—a limestone area characterized by sinkholes, underground streams and caverns. The entire county is underlaid with St. Louis limestone, which in many places has eroded away, leaving the area from Valmeyer to Columbia and Waterloo honeycombed with caverns and surface sinkholes. Caverns are created by naturally acidic water flowing through and dissolving limestone. As the surface limestone collapses into the caves, dry sinkholes begin to pock the surface ground. At times, the sinkholes are plugged by sediment and become small round lakes as water collects in them. You will see several of these pools along the road between Waterloo and Wartburg. If you're interested in caving, **Illinois Caverns** at Burksville, southeast of Wartburg on KK Road, are open to cavers (or spelunkers) with proper equipment. They offer three miles of walking passages and some mineral formations.

A BRIEF HISTORY OF MONROE COUNTY

The history of towns along the Great River Road in Monroe County is distinct from the Colonial French history of Randolph County to the south. Columbia, Waterloo, and several other towns including nearby Whiteside and Smithton began as colonial American settlements. Piggot's Fort became Columbia and Peterstown and Belle Fontaine conjoined to become modern-day Waterloo.

The founders of these towns—Moore, Ogle, Ramsey, Piggott, and Peters—were all Revolutionary War veterans who had helped claim the area for the Americans under the command of George Rogers Clark. Land grants from this area, afterward known as the Illinois Military Tract, were awarded to many veterans of the Revolutionary War—the first time the new country offered compensation to its veterans.

Columbia, Illinois
Population 4269

Columbia, like most cities within 30 miles of St. Louis, has become a bedroom community of subdivisions. The historic districts are still intact, just awash in the modern jumble of life. Columbia's older section is east on Main Street, clustered around the Catholic Church. The **Gund-**

INSIGHT

George Rogers Clark and His Long Knives

Clark is considered to be the conqueror of the Old Northwest during the War of Independence. His "battles" in Kaskaskia and Cahokia were among the furthest west of the Revolutionary War.

Clark and his troops, known as the Virginia Long Knives, landed at old Fort Masac on the Ohio River in 1778. They marched north to Kaskaskia, liberating the town from British control on July 4 of 1778. Encouraged by their parish priest, Father Pierre Gibault, French citizens joined Clark's soldiers to march north to Prairie du Rocher and onward to Cahokia. In each town, the British surrendered without a battle. In 1779, Clark marched from Kaskaskia to Vincennes, where he again defeated the British. He claimed the new territory for the Commonwealth of Virginia.

When Virginia ceded the Illinois territory to the fledgling U.S. government, Thomas Jefferson granted each veteran of the Revolutionary War 400 acres of land in the new territory. By 1790 the area was organized as the Northwest Territory under Arthur St. Clair, with its capital in Marietta, Ohio.

lach House at 625 Main and several more Civil War era houses still stand.

Columbia, landlocked at the top of the bluffs, has several claims to fame. The SS *Columbia* was named for this small town. It's also the hometown of two Navy Admirals, Admiral Carlyle Trost, Rear Admiral under President George Bush, and Admiral John Weinel. A third full Admiral, John Wendt, grew up in nearby Millstadt.

COLUMBIA'S FOUNDER, JAMES PIGGOT

Captain James Piggott, a native of North Carolina, first saw these river bluffs as a soldier under George Rogers Clark. After the Revolutionary War, Piggott settled in Jefferson, Tennessee. When that settlement was besieged by Indians, Piggot remembered the French settlements along the Mississippi, moved to Kaskaskia and married (his third or fourth marriage) a French woman who had been abandoned by her husband and left with five children. They moved upriver to establish a port on the American Bottoms between the bluffs and the river.

In the late 1780s, Piggot built a fort—actually 17 cabins in a square around a large barn—as protection from raiding Indians. The barn site, now called Piggot's Fort, has been discovered, and its rotting timbers have been carbon-dated to 1792. The cabin foundations may well lie under eight feet of silt in the flood plain between Columbia and the river.

Piggott was named a judge under Arthur St. Clair and started a ferry service between East St. Louis and St. Louis. A street in East St. Louis is named Piggott Avenue in his honor.

INDIAN/AMERICAN RELATIONS

The American settlers at the upper end of the American Bottom did not have the same harmonious relations with the native Indians as did the French and Illini Indian tribes. There were frequent run-ins among settlers, native Indians, and such northern tribes as the Sac, Mesquakie, Kickapoo, and Potawatomie. The book *Annals of the West* relates the following story from Columbia about an area still known today as Andy's Run. It was a run that James Andrews hoped, wrongly, would draw the Indians away from his young family.

> In 1786, the Kickapoo Indians attacked the American settlements and killed James Andrews. His pregnant wife and two daughters were taken prisoner by the Indians. His wife and one daughter died on the trail. French traders ransomed the second daughter. The Indians had previously threatened the settlement, and the people had built and entered a blockhouse; but this family was out and defenseless.

—— O ——

Continue to Waterloo on Hwy. 3.

Waterloo, Illinois
Population 4646

The Colonial American roots of Waterloo are apparent from its square downtown commons area. The **Waterloo Historic District** is on the National Register of Historic Places and includes many of the 200 nineteenth century buildings still standing in Waterloo. The west side of Main Street is remarkable in that only two of sixteen structures date from the twentieth century. German heritage is also apparent—in *streethouses,* their front doors right at the sidewalk. A weekly free band concert is offered at the Pavilion in Courthouse Yard. Konarcik City Park (D) is east of the city limits. Koenigsmark City Park has a public swimming pool.

A BRIEF HISTORY OF WATERLOO

Peter Rogers (1795-1859) came to the area from Massachusetts to settle five acres at the north end of today's Waterloo. He called his settlement Peter's Town. Rogers operated a general store, gristmill, woolen mill, brickyard, quarry, rope factory, cider mill and more. His primary markets were St. Louis and New Orleans. His father was chaplain to George Washington during the Revolutionary War.

WHAT TO SEE IN WATERLOO

Waterloo Winery (A)

Along Route 3, near the northern entrance to the city. 725 N. Market Street. Open by appointment. 618-939-8339.

Bring your own picnic lunch or barbecue and eat at shaded picnic tables on the grounds. Wine tasting and free tours by appointment. Cobblestones near the patio came from the levees at St. Louis and East St. Louis. Highly recommended is a refreshing, sparkly non-alcoholic peach drink.

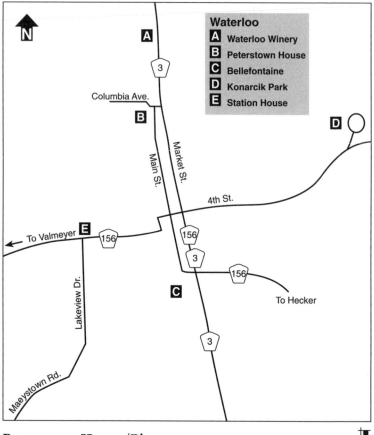

Peterstown House (B)

Just off Route 3 at 275 N. Main. 618-458-6422. Free.

The Peterstown House was built in the 1830s as a stage-coach stop on the Kaskaskia-Cahokia Trail, which passed by the front door. Notice the limestone curbing along the road. There are two log homes behind the home; on one leans a water trough carved from a log. Indians and settlers made their boats or dugouts in a very similar manner.

The Kaskaskia Trail is noted on French maps as early as 1796, when two trails were indicated, one on top of the bluff and one below. The upland route (through Belle Fontaine) would have been more reliable and is considered to be the actual trail. The Trail followed Indian and pre-historic trails between the French-Indian settlements at

Cahokia and those at Kaskaskia. Both Belle Fontaine (see below) and Peter's Town were located along the Trail. The only part of the original trail that is still preserved stretches south and uphill between the old Belle Fontaine farm and the new homes to its east. Walk the grassy pathway to the Revolutionary War era cemetery at the top of the hill. It is open for those who would like to try stone rubbings.

Bellefontaine (C)

Just off Route 3 at the intersection with Highway 156. Follow signs to the log cabin, brick home and historic marker.

Belle Fontaine, the original name for the southern part of Waterloo, commemorates the settlement by the Captain James Moore family in 1782 at this location. The fountain that gave the settlement its name still flows below the hill behind the brick house.

Those who first stayed at Moore's Belle Fontaine included Shadrach Bond, Sr., Larken Rutherford, James Garretson, and Robert Kidd, all of whom moved on to start their own settlements. Rogers and Moore joked that if Moore's Belle Fontaine and Rogers' Peter's Town ever met, it would be their Waterloo. Thus, the conjoined town became Waterloo.

Vera Kohlmeier from the Waterloo Historical Society recalled that as a young girl she would stand in the yard of the brick home at Bellefontaine and admire fields all around the house that were full of blossoming apple orchards. A well-house was built over the spring, and milk, cheese, and meats were kept cool there. Her mother and grandparents lived in this house, and Vera remembers the arrowheads her mother spoke of finding there as a child. There are early records of frequent Indian attacks in *The Illinois History of 1876*:

> *1787—La Belle Fontaine is a small stockade inhabited altogether by ... almost entirely by immigrants from Kentucky and Virginia..*
>
> *Early in this year, five families near Belle Fontaine united and built a blockhouse and surrounded it with palisades*

in which these families resided. While laboring in the cornfield they were obliged to carry their rifles, and often at night had to keep guard. Under these embarrassments, and in daily alarm, they cultivated their cornfields.

According to this history, Indian attacks seemed to become more frequent and virulent in the fall, thus they became know as "Indian Summers."

SPECIAL EVENTS IN WATERLOO

May (4th Sunday): *Belle Fontaine Quilt Show*

July (Sunday after the 4th): *Classic Car Show*

— ⚙ —

Return to Hwy. 156 toward Valmeyer. Turn toward Wartburg on the Maeystown Road just beyond the Station House at the edge of town. Note the sink hole lakes scattered among the housing developments outside of town.

Just beyond the church in Wartburg, the fields become woods, and the road begins winding downward. A settlement appears and we cross the one-lane stone bridge of ...

INSIGHT

Sunflowers in Illinois

During my October visit, the field opposite the Stone Church at Wartburg was abloom in sunflowers! Eighteen species of sunflower, thirteen of them native, have been found growing in Illinois. The annual sunflower was introduced from the central plains and reaches about 10 feet high. This is the plant domesticated by Native Americans to become the cultivated sunflower.

A second sunflower used by the Indians for food is the Jerusalem Artichoke, or "Indian potato." This perennial sends out long runners which end in large edible tubers. As indicated by its name, it has since been cultivated around the world, including the Middle East. The plant is a native of Illinois.

Maeystown, Illinois

Population 130

Maeystown is perched midway between table-flat bottoms and rolling upland plains at a point where three streams flow down a ragged hillside. Like the village of Elsah, Illinois, north of Alton, (see Volume 2 of *Discover! America's Great River Road*) Maeystown is notable for its limestone and brick buildings dating from the 1850s. Like Elsah, the entire town is on the National Register of Historic Places.

Stop and visit the former gristmill, now the **Maeystown Visitor and Interpretive Center**. Walk the flagstone-guttered streets to the **stone church** atop the hill. Some of the limestone curbing and gutters are 150 years old. Each block extends two feet underground and weighs 250 pounds. The original log church, the stone bridge and various outbuildings, barns and smokehouses comprise more than 60 historically significant buildings in the village.

The **Corner George Inn** offers sumptuous accommodations. Innkeepers Dave and Marcia Braswell chose the unique name because four George Hoffmans lived in a row down Main Street between 1907 and 1914. To keep them straight, locals bestowed upon each a nickname: Laughing George, Fat George, Schmitt (or Blacksmith) George and (yep!) Corner George! Gift shops, sweet treats, noon meals, antiques, and pottery are available at several of the restored buildings. For travel information, or to schedule a tour or accommodations, call 618-458-6660.

I arrived late in the evening to silent streets, the insistent, repetitive song of frogs, and the zeep zeep of cicadas. I sat at the park bench at the bottom of Main Street beside the stream enjoying the quiet sounds when suddenly in the gathering darkness, I was startled to hear the wild cackle of what sounded like a cross between a monkey and a kookaburra! The barred owl, I'm told later, is well known for its weird and varied repertoire!

"Maeystown from On High." Painting by Charles H. Wallis.

A BRIEF HISTORY OF MAEYSTOWN
AND THE GERMAN FORTY-EIGHTERS

Adapted from The Significance of the Village of Maeystown, Illinois, *by Gloria Bundy*

Fifty-six years after Captain James Moore settled his family at Belle Fontaine, Jacob Maeys bought the acreage along three streams near today's Maeysville as a site for his sawmill. Maeys purchased his 100 acres just ahead of the great influx of Germans called the Forty-Eighters, who streamed up the Mississippi River from ports in New Orleans. More than people of any other nationality, the Germans populated and developed the towns of the mid-nineteenth century. These were merchants and craftsmen, well-educated and highly principled families who left Germany to avoid political revolution and religious, economic, and military oppression during the years 1848 through 1854.

The immigrants brought with them a knowledge of stone and brick masonry and solid building construction techniques. The surrounding limestone hills provided stonemasons with material for buildings, bridges, and retaining walls. Many of the stone structures standing in Maeystown were built using mortarless masonry. Bricks were also man-ufactured using the clay soil that prevails here.

These early Germans were virtually self-sufficient and interacted very little with their colonial Yankee neighbors. For a long period of time, including the World War I years, antagonism between the two groups ran high and included various raids between the Yankees and the "damn Dutch" and their neighbors. Throughout World War I, the inhabitants of Maeystown held to their customs, language and traditions. In 1929 the last church confirmations were offered in German, and during World War II, use of the Ger-man language was discontinued in the churches altogether.

SPECIAL EVENTS IN MAEYSTOWN

Tuesday before Ash Wednesday: *Fastnacht,* German pan-cake & sausage dinner, St. John Church.

April, last Sunday: *Fruhlingsfest,* Maeystown Springfest. Volksmarch and crafters fair.

October, 2nd Sunday: *Oktoberfest,* Mill St. German eth-nic craft festival with ethnic food and family fun, 618-458-6930.

The Corner George Inn, Maeystown.

Gloria (Maeys) Bundy
Monroe County Historian

Gloria Bundy, the granddaughter of founder Jacob Maeys, lives in her home beside his original one-room log cabin. For much of her life she has been an historian extraordinaire for Monroe County.

As we muse at the railing of her deck, Indian summer rests brilliantly upon the rocky outcroppings in glorious reds and yellows.

The stream that attracted Jacob Maeys to the site still ripples along merrily over bedrock limestone. The site of the original spring is visible in the yard, but an earth tremor redirected the water to an opening further away. We poke around in the log cabin, now a "dog-trot," meaning that a second room was added beside the first, with a covered corridor between. Gloria is trying to keep up the old buildings and recently restored a built-in iron kettle on a brick oven for heating water on washday.

"I'd like to restore the whole cabin," she tells me, "but there are not public funds for private buildings. So I do what I can."

Later, driving through the table-flat cornfields between the bluffs and the river, I ask Gloria about her experiences during the flood of 1993.

"What I remember most," she says, "was driving to a spot along the bluff that looked over our acreage below. I will never forget seeing only water as far as the eye could see, except for here and there a rooftop. The devastation was complete. Many homes and four towns were washed completely away.

"The silence was so deep, so pervasive. No birds called, no frogs, no crickets. We later motored a boat over our cornfield. The depth finder said twelve feet. A woodpile poked out of the water and I remember it was absolutely covered

Continued on next page

with tiny frogs. It was like a Biblical plague! Then as the water dried up, the mosquitoes came. There was an audible roar over the entire valley. The hum of hordes of mosquitoes!

"The saddest part of the flood was watching the evacuations during the four weeks before the flood. Families loaded all their belongings onto trucks. There were long lines of trucks leaving the deserted homes and towns. And there was nothing to come back to after water had inundated the houses for two months. We had a house down there. Two of the walls were just gone."

As we follow Maeystown Road down the hill to Bluff Road and drive toward Valmeyer, Gloria continues her story.

"The railroad levees were under water. Any homes we see now were up to their porch roofs in water. Many were under water. Some homes were repaired with flood insurance dollars, some were bought out and destroyed by the government.

"Most towns on the bottoms were built about 1902 when the railroad came through. The quarries shipped rock by rail and there was lots of work in the quarries. It hadn't flooded down here in 99 years at the time Fults and Valmeyer were built. But 1993 was the fourth devastating flood that I've seen since 1943. The first was in 1943, then '44, then '47. Now it's flooded in both '93 and '95. The lucky thing about all these floods is that no one was ever killed."

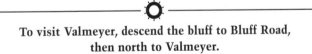

To visit Valmeyer, descend the bluff to Bluff Road,
then north to Valmeyer.

Valmeyer, Illinois

At this moment, there are two Valmeyers. The one below the hill is just a fragment of its pre-flood self. Streets lined with light poles lead nowhere; telephone poles and a few houses still stand. A car repair shop seems to be the only sign of life. No sign designates this as "old"

Valmeyer. Its citizens—600 of the 900 who populated the old town—have moved en masse to a new Valmeyer up on the bluff. Its brand new $12 million dollar school services a community which is developing house by house, month by month.

○

Follow Bluff Road south from Valmeyer to Fults.

Alternatively, **follow Hwy. 156 west to Levee Rd. and ride the gravel-topped river levee to Ivy Rd., which also will take you to Fults.**

Harrisonville may be marked on your map along Highway 156 just before the junction of 156 and Levee Road. Most of the town, however, was swept away during the flood of 1993—the end of a long retreat from its original 1780 location on the banks of the river. **Levee Road** is a rough gravel byway used mostly by farm trucks hauling grain to the grain elevator on the Mississippi River at Outlet Road about halfway between Valmeyer and Fults. This is a convenient opportunity to drive atop a Mississippi River levee. If you turn in at the grain elevator on Outlet Road, you can have a peek at the main river channel ... and you'll be able to note the water level mark for the flood of 1993 on the main silo.

The river side of the levee is mostly wet bottomland crowded with the skeletal remains of downed and dead trees. Many oaks and hickories drowned during the 1993 and 1995 floods because the water was so high for so long, damage that is apparent along much of the Great River Road. Pecan trees appear to have fared the best.

Fults, Illinois

Fults, too, is only a flood-washed relic of a village. We followed a pattern of empty streets to rejoin Bluff Road.

WHAT TO SEE NEAR FULTS

Fults Hill Prairie Nature Preserve

The Preserve, located near the former village of Fults along Bluff Road, is very small but pleasant, with about three miles of hiking trails, two of which are immediately accessible from the small parking/picnic area.

The hillside prairie offers travelers an opportunity to explore some natural terrain quite different from the domesticated cornfields alongside Levee Road. The trails are steep and this is prime copperhead territory, so watch your step.

Three plant communities thrive in this small preserve. Forests are mainly on dry sites with species such as black oak, post oak, and black hickory. Ravine forests and other shaded moist areas include white oak, red oak, chinquapin oak, sugar maple and hickories. Hill prairies on the steeper bluffs include big and little bluestem, Indian grass and side-oats grama and wildflowers such as blazing stars, coneflowers, asters, and goldenrod. Controlled burning is practiced to maintain natural prairie areas. Limestone glades shelter shorter and sparser vegetation than that found on the hill prairies.

Kidd Lake Marsh Natural Area

This lowland marsh in the bottoms below Fults Hill is dominated by cattails, lotus, smartweed (so named because it is a stinging plant—it "smarts," like nettle) and cord grass. Migrating waterfowl are dependent on these small remnant patches of the huge marshes and wetlands that once covered, and helped to create, today's rich agricultural bottomlands.

The limestone used in the thick walls of the original French Fort de Chartres was quarried from neighboring bluffs and skidded across frozen Kidd Lake to the fort construction site at the river's edge. A small population of venomous cottonmouth snakes is isolated in Kidd Lake, the northernmost range of the cottonmouth in Illinois. The main population begins 50 miles to the south.

Just south of Fults on Bluff Road, a sign announcing **Trapper's Falls, Fish and Fur** points east up a gravel road. Here is an unusual opportunity to fish for an 80-pound flathead catfish, or paddlefish! Gene and Gilsela Esker maintain 11 fish ponds that do double duty as holding tanks and fishing ponds.

INSIGHT

Gene Esker, Fisherman and Trapper

"In the spring," Gene explains, "everyone is catching fish and the fish market is flooded. I sell what I can and put the rest in the holding ponds. When I need them later to fill orders, I just take them out of the ponds. Meantime, some of them just sit there and eat. They get pretty big and provide a real thrill at the end of a fishing pole."

The fur trade and fish cleaning all take place in a handsome log cabin beside his home. "You can't trade furs in a new building," he explained. "You gotta do it proper." He built the log cabin in 1984, but Gene has been called "Trapper" since his school days.

"My dad trapped this whole area, and his dad trapped when he was a kid. But not my kid. I won't allow it. It's hard work and it only nets about $1 an hour. People might think it's a romantic life, but it's too hard for what you get back."

Gene is a riverman, with a big grin and plenty of stories. "I had a baby beaver that I rescued from a trap. It liked to crawl into our laps for a cuddle, just like a kitten. He sucked milk from pieces of bread until he was big enough to escape. Then he hung out with the dogs and would keep coming to the house for his milk and bread. Then he got into my ponds. He was about 60 pounds and attracted two other beavers. They cut at least 150 trees up there. Everything from the saplings to the monster trees. I had to destroy the three beavers."

With a little prompting, Gene rattled off his personal fishing bests: 1600 pounds of catfish caught in ten minutes (with a net through the ice); 700 pounds of paddlefish in ten minutes. He fishes with basket traps, trammel nets, and hoop nets—most of them hanging on the cabin walls (see page 221).

In 1988 he caught 500 snapping turtles in 12 trips out. I ask to see the turtle tank, because there's few critters as nasty looking as a good-sized snapper. Gene duly impressed me by confidently reaching into the dark water. He missed several grabs and then decided to use a net.

"If I lose a finger I won't be able to clean fish for a while," he told me as he untangled an angry snapper from his net.

Gene says the bluff area is prime territory for copperheads. He's only seen one cottonmouth in his life, though he says black water snakes are often mistaken for cottonmouths. Water snakes are basically harmless, but they can reach eight inches in diameter and will "bite the heck out of you" if you try to handle them.

"Copperheads," Gene tells me, "are dangerous because they just lay there, sunning or under leaves or logs. They don't move or try to escape you. You don't even know it's there until it bites you without any warning. Watch where you step, or you're a fool"

Chapters 5 and 6 contain information about the Colonial French Districts on either side of the Mississippi River. Access Ste. Genevieve (Chapter 5) via U.S. Hwy 61 or I-55 on the Missouri side or via the Modoc Ferry from the Illinois shore. To continue south along Bluff Road toward Prairie du Rocher, IL, see page 75, Chapter 6.

Ste. Genevieve County,
Missouri

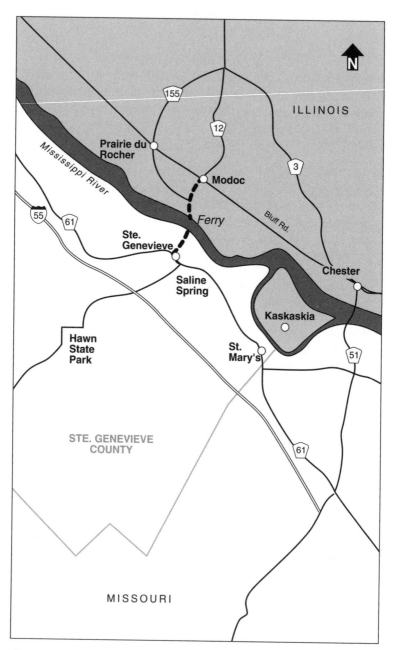

5

Ste. Genevieve County, Missouri

Ste. Genevieve, Missouri
Population 4,000

The French enthusiast has already discovered that for all the historic impact of the French along the Mississippi River, very little of the French culture remains. Yet nowhere along the river is it more palpable than in Ste. Genevieve and its sister sites in the Illinois French Colonial District. Some might suggest that a half-day visit is about right for a small village like Ste. Genevieve, but that would be at a great loss to the traveler. Settle in at an historic bed & breakfast, walk the village streets, take the Modoc Car Ferry to Fort de Chartres in Illinois, soak up some history, and enjoy this great national treasure!

Our home for several days was the **Southern Hotel** at the corner of Market and Third streets (800-275-1412 or 573-883-3493). Owners Barb and Mike Hankins are justifiably proud of the restoration and interior decoration of the hotel. Barb is an artist at heart and visitors benefit from her tasteful displays of fans, coins, and butter molds that decorate the rooms and the dining table. The artwork blends seamlessly with the restoration project: hand-painted door frames, colorful handpainted tubs, and a tiny gift shop tucked into a garden ablaze with flowers.

The village abounds in historic buildings restored as bed & breakfast inns and gift shops. **The Inn St. Gemme de Beauvais** (1848) is at the north end of Main Street, on the way to the Modoc Ferry. In 1948 it became the first B & B in the state of Missouri (800-818-5744 or 573-883-5744).

Other recommended B&Bs include the **Creole House B&B** (800-275-6041 or 573-883-7171); the **Main Street Inn** built in the 1880s (800-918-9199); and the **Steiger Haus**, a family B&B noted for murder mystery evenings and hosted by an eleventh generation native of Ste. Genevieve (800-814-5881 or 573-883-5881).

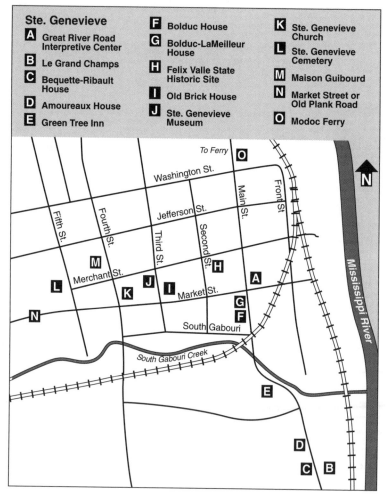

Ste. Genevieve

- **A** Great River Road Interpretive Center
- **B** Le Grand Champs
- **C** Bequette-Ribault House
- **D** Amoureaux House
- **E** Green Tree Inn
- **F** Bolduc House
- **G** Bolduc-LaMeilleur House
- **H** Felix Valle State Historic Site
- **I** Old Brick House
- **J** Ste. Genevieve Museum
- **K** Ste. Genevieve Church
- **L** Ste. Genevieve Cemetery
- **M** Maison Guibourd
- **N** Market Street or Old Plank Road
- **O** Modoc Ferry

The Mississippi is generally nowhere in sight, having deserted this once-thriving port city to devour the hapless village of Kaskaskia on the opposite shore. I say "generally," because during the flood of 1993, Ste. Genevieve's citizens struggled to hastily build earthen levees to hold back a river that seemed intent on encircling and swallowing up the village. Sixteen thousand truckloads of dirt and gravel and $25,000 worth of plastic were used to build the levees. On August 6, 1993, the river crested at 49.67 feet, 6 feet above the previous record set in 1973, when waters encroached upon Washington and Third Streets.

A brochure from Ste. Genevieve recalls a saying: "When God divided the water and the land, He had water left over. He turned it loose and told it to go wherever it wanted to; and that was the Mississippi River. It still goes wherever it wants to." (See levee photograph on p. 233.)

A BRIEF HISTORY OF STE. GENEVIEVE

Antoine de la Mothe Cadillac was one of the first Frenchmen to explore this area on behalf of the French Company of the West between 1713 and 1717. It is believed that he dug a pit looking for silver in the area now known as Mine La Motte, but left the area when all he found was lead ore.

In 1723 François Phillipe Renault opened lead mines in what is now known as Washington County. His small band of 13 white and 22 black men mined Mine La Motte and established the village of St. Phillipe outside the gates of the first Fort de Chartres.

Reports indicate that the Company of the West began bringing black slaves into the area, mainly from the island of Haiti. By 1746, 300 French settlers, 600 black slaves, and more than 100 Indian slaves were living in French Illinois. Most families, even the very poor, had one to three slaves. To be "French" in these early days often meant not only that one was born of French stock, but also that one was a *metis* or mix of French, Indian, and Caribbean or

The Flood of 1993

AUG 7.'72
49.67'

STE.
GENEVIEVE
TEN
WORST
FLOODS

APR 30'73
43.30'

JUNE 1844
41.39'

JULY 1951
40.28'
JULY 1947
40.26'
APR 7.'73
39.80'
OCT.11.'86
39.20'
APR 44 31.14
MAY '43
38.94'
DEC.'82
38.50'

March 10, the National Weather Service predicts below normal precipitation for the summer.

June 10, a high pressure system stalled in the southeast and forced Gulf air to move north, hitting cool northwest air. The first 8-inch rainstorms begin in the Dakotas, Wisconsin, and Minnesota.

June 20, the first dam burst on the Black River, a tributary entering the Mississippi at La Crosse, Wisconsin. One hundred homes were submerged to their rooftops in western Wisconsin. The upper 200 miles of the Mississippi were closed to river traffic.

July 8, a "boil" order went into effect for all water use in Ste. Genevieve and continued until late September.

July 10, the bridge over the Mississippi at Fort Madison in southern Iowa was closed. The area had experienced rain for 54 of 58 days. 830 miles of river were closed between Cairo, Illinois, and St. Paul, Minnesota. More than 100 rivers feeding into the Mississippi flooded by July 14.

August 2, the river crested at 49'7" in St. Louis. Enough water was flowing under Eads Bridge to fill Busch stadium every 65 seconds.

August 24, the Mississippi River locks reopened to commercial river traffic. The flood's overall impact: failure of 150 primary and secondary levees, twelve billion dollars in damages, 48 deaths, and nine states involved. By July 15th, every area of the river had had at least twice its normal rainfall; some had had six times as much.

A board outside of Ste. Genevieve records high water marks of historic floods.

African blood. White women were a rarity in the wilderness outposts before 1740.

In 1752, Ste. Genevieve had only 23 residents. Homes were small, built of sturdy square vertical logs (walnut, oak or cedar), and whitewashed inside and out, with a *galerie* porch on all four sides. The central part of the roof was steeply pointed [double-pitched] so that snow could not accumulate—a neat trick learned from French Canadians—while the galerie porch was a Caribbean touch introduced by the southern French. Stockades of pointed vertical logs encircled the homes to keep free-ranging animals and hostile Indians away. Tiny dirt "yards" between the stockade fence and the houses were intended as firebreaks and were swept free of sticks and leaves.

After the British defeat of the French ended the French and Indian War in 1763, the population of Ste. Genevieve swelled to 600 as French residents from Kaskaskia on the east bank moved west into what they believed was French territory. Shortly afterward, flooding forced the first villagers to move further up St. Mary's Road (the King's Highway), near where the Bequette-Ribault (1778) and Amoureaux houses (late 18th century) still stand.

WHAT TO SEE IN STE. GENEVIEVE

Great River Road Interpretive Center (A)　　　⌐

66 South Main. Open 9:00 a.m. to 3 p.m. weekdays and 9 a.m. to 4 p.m. on weekends. Call for information on accommodations and special events, 573-883-7096.

My visit to Ste. Genevieve began at the Great River Road Interpretive Center. Displays and dioramas offer an overview of the history of the French and their battles with a strong-willed river. As wood was harvested from riverbanks to fuel the steamboats' boilers, the banks became unstable, eroding into the main channel. This resulted in a wide, shallow river whose sandbars, shoals, and snags made travel treacherous. It is estimated that by 1870 there had been an average of one steamboat wreck per mile for the 200 miles between St. Louis and the Ohio River at Cairo.

Le Grand Champs (The Big Field) (B)

This is the site of Old Ste. Genevieve (Le Vieux Village), three miles south of the Interpretive Center along St. Mary's Road.

The inhabitants of the original village of Ste. Genevieve, settled between 1725 and 1740, built along the riverbank. Their houses and outbuildings backed onto the 3000 acres of Le Grand Champs.

Today, only the "big field" remains, surrounded by low bluffs. There are no fences in this vast acreage, but old pecan trees called "marker trees" still separate one farmer's long, narrow field *(longlot)* from another's. The French built neither homes nor fences on their acreages, yet each field, like a homesite in the village, was individually owned.

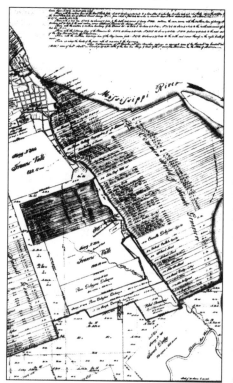

The European tradition of longlots *(champs en long)* was ideally suited to the river environment that early settlers found in the New World because it allowed each farmer access to the river. The long fields were used throughout the French historic district and along Canada's St.

1815 map of the "longlots" around Ste. Genevieve.

Lawrence Seaway. French settlements along the Upper Mississippi River (in Prairie du Chien, Wisconsin and on French Island near La Crosse, Wisconsin) also show evidence of these longlots.

St. Mary's Road follows a portion of the old King's Highway or *El Camino Real*. Already well-traveled by 1789, it was established by the Spanish as the land portion of a river-and-land route for government and ecclesiastical communication in the French district. Couriers left New Orleans by boat and followed the Mississippi River until they reached New Madrid, where they switched to this land route. Missouri's Great River Road parallels the same route today.

Mississippian Indian Mounds

Along St. Mary's Road.

From my vantage point overlooking a bare spring field, the remnants of a large Indian mound located along St. Mary's road was clearly visible.

"Actually, there are five mounds," explained Rob Beckerman, my guide. Only after he pointed this out did it become apparent that several smaller mounds encircled the larger one I had seen at first. In 1941 the large mound was reported to be 30 feet high and encircled by eight mounds. It is only half that size now and has probably

Mississippian Indian mound, St. Mary's Road, Ste. Genevieve.

67

shrunk considerably during the past two hundred years; so it is very likely that this was once a large temple or platform mound supporting a building, rather than a signal or burial mound.

It is believed that the Mississippian culture was born in the fertile, floodwater-enriched soil of the American Bottom between St. Louis and Ste. Genevieve. More than 28,000 mounds have been identified in the state of Missouri. Look for similar mounds to appear about every eight miles along the Great River Road.

HISTORIC HOMES

The hallmark of Ste. Genevieve is its historic homes. They are such a treasure that the federal government is building a forty-million-dollar levee to protect the ancient homes from floods in the foreseeable future.

The Bequette-Ribault House (C)

St. Mary's Road. Available for exterior viewing only.

This house dates to 1778, and is one of four known surviving structures in North America of *poteaux en terre* (post-in-the ground) construction. Like the Amoureaux House (see

Amoureax House—The pointed roof and broad galerie porch are typical of historic homes.

below), it sits on its original site and was probably a farm house. Note how the roof is elevated from the main walls to allow heat to escape in the summer.

The Amoureaux House (D)

St. Mary's Road. Available for exterior viewing only.

Built late in the 18th century by a member of the St. Gemme de Beauvais family and later occupied by French nobleman Mathurin Michael Amoureaux, an acquaintance of Thomas Jefferson. It is also of *poteaux en terre* construction and was originally thatched.

The Green Tree Inn (E)

On Gabouri Creek.

Built after flooding in 1785 forced villagers to build on higher ground. It is considered to be Ste. Genevieve's oldest inn. It was built in 1789 by Nicholas Janis, a friend of George Rogers Clark.

By 1810 there were ten working lead mines, a salt works on Saline Creek, a pottery kiln and several mills in the area. One of the mills was owned by Moses Austin. When hard times came, he and son Stephen moved onto a Texas

Green Tree Inn, overlooking Gabouri Creek. Note the high water mark on the pole at right.

land grant. Their cabin was located behind the low-water bridge opposite the Green Tree Inn on Gabouri Creek.

Bolduc House (F) ᛏ

Opposite the Great River Road Interpretive Center at Market and Main Streets. Open between April and November. Admission charge.

Built in 1770 and moved to its present site in 1785. It is considered to be the finest restored Creole house in the nation. Note especially the vertical log construction with its thick mortar and the small dirt firebreak yard.

Louis Bolduc was Ste. Genevieve's richest citizen. A French Canadian merchant, he joined forces with Menard and Valle after the arrival of the first steamboat in 1817.

Bolduc-LeMeilleur House (G) ᛏ

Opposite the Great River Road Interpretive Center at Market and Main Streets. Open weekends April through November and daily June 1 through September 1. Admission charge.

Next door to the Bolduc House, the Bolduc-LeMeilleur was built in 1820 by a grandson-in-law of Louis Bolduc. The architecture is a combination of French and American influences.

Felix Valle State Historic Site (H) ᛏ

Merchant and Second Streets. Open year-round. Admission charge.

My guide pointed out that many of the homes at this intersection date from 1790, 1823, and 1868, but have been comfortably remodeled. Clues to recognizing the historic homes include pointed roof lines and closed-in galerie porches.

The Felix Valle House, built in 1818, is transitional from the early French to the new Federal style introduced by the Americans. It was occupied by Felix and Odile Valle, half as a residence and half as a mercantile headquarters for the Menard & Valle trade firm that controlled the Valle lead mines and the Indian Trade in Missouri and

Arkansas. François Valle, Felix's grandfather, came to the area from French Canada in 1748. Jean Baptiste Valle, Felix's father, was the last commandant of Ste. Genevieve; his house still stands at Market and Main, though it is privately owned.

Old Brick House (I)

Third and Market Streets. It is now a restaurant that can be visited during regular business hours.

Today's historic village is the second village of Ste. Genevieve. Most of its commercial brick buildings were built by German immigrants after 1805; before that year, bricks had to be hauled upriver. The Old Brick House (1804) is the only French brick building. It survived the New Madrid Earthquake in 1811-12.

Ste. Genevieve Museum (J)

Dubourg and Merchant Streets. Open daily. Small admission charge.

The museum contains many local memorabilia, including prehistoric Indian relics, old documents and artifacts, and an intact salt evaporating bowl found at Saline Spring.

Ste. Genevieve Church and Cemetery (K, L)

Merchant and Fourth Streets.

Three different church buildings on this site have served Ste. Genevieve's congregation. The original log church was moved from *Le Grand Champs* to this site in 1794. It was replaced by a stone church in 1838. A new church was begun in 1876 and built around the old stone church, which was removed after the new church was finished in 1880. The foundation stones of the 1838 church help support the central floor of the new church. The paintings in the church were gifts from King Louis XV of France and date from before 1769. The historic cemetery at Fifth and Market dates from 1787 and commemorates many of the earliest settlers.

Maison Guibourd-Valle House (M)

Fourth and Market Streets. Admission charge.

Built about 1799 by a French settler, this house is elegantly restored, and like many of the other historic homes boasts a Norman truss and hand-hewn beams of oak and/or walnut.

Market Street or the Old Plank Road (N)

Work on Market Street began in 1851 to accommodate traffic from the iron and lead mines of Iron Mountain and for farmers bringing goods to market. The 42-mile-long roadway was built of 2-inch-thick planks cut from nearby forests.

Modern Highway 32 parallels the same route today. Notice that toward the intersection with U.S. Highway 61, neighboring bluffs appear to have been mined. In fact, the lime quarries are all underground, and the rocky hills we see are scrap from the mines. The first hand-fired lime kiln was developed in 1840. Today, the Mississippi Lime Company is the largest employer in Ste. Genevieve and operates the second-largest limestone quarry in the world.

Hawn State Park

Off Highway 32 on Highway 144 in Ste. Genevieve County. Hiking, picnicking, and camping.

This is considered to be one of Missouri's most beautiful and unspoiled landscapes, an excellent example of Missouri's eastern Ozark sandstone country. A 10-mile backpacking trail winds along Pickle Creek and the River Aux Vases.

The Modoc Ferry (O)

North end of Main Street. The round trip ticket for car and occupants is about $10. Flash your car lights to call the ferry from the opposite shore. The ferry leaves on its first crossing from Ste. Genevieve at about 6 a.m. and returns to Ste. Genevieve for the evening at about 5:45 p.m. It makes the crossing every 10 or 20 minutes during the day.

The Modoc Ferry offers the visitor a rare opportunity to experience a boat crossing of the Main Channel of the Mississippi River. Crossing by ferry here will also save about a 23-mile drive to the next downriver bridge near Chester, Illinois. The current here is very strong. When combined with a brisk wind, it is a challenging crossing even for an experienced pilot!

Fishing off the rocks near the ferry ramp is especially good when catfish gather to feed on corn blown into the river as barges are loaded nearby. Black long-necked cormorants are abundant in the area and are often mistaken for geese when they travel along the river in great V-shaped flocks. The cormorants are fish-eaters that were long regarded as a threat to commercial fishing and slaughtered by commercial fishermen. Now protected by law, they are repopulating the river valley.

———————— ⚙ ————————

Take the Modoc Ferry to the Illinois shore.
Continue toward the village of Modoc, Illinois,
at the base of a tall rock wall.

Much of Levee Road's blacktop surface is on top of or beside the levee. It is hard to imagine that the Mississippi would ever breech this high earthen wall, but in 1993 the swollen river lapped at the very top.

———————— ⚙ ————————

From Modoc, turn north on Bluff Road to visit the French
Illinois Colonial District or south for the Modoc Rock
Shelter and the home of Pierre Menard.

Randolph County,
Illinois

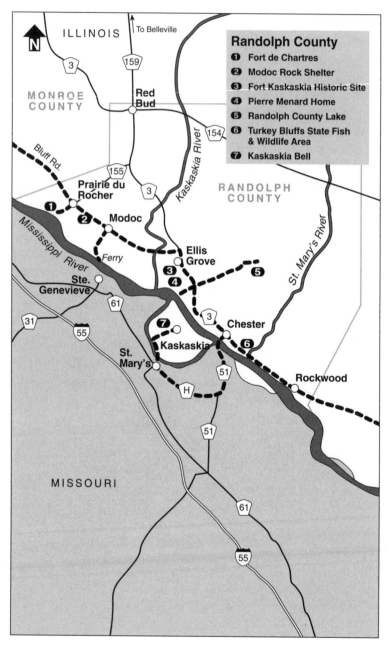

6

Randolph County, Illinois

In Randolph County, history sings loudly to the traveler. At a time when New York was a struggling village, French settlements were springing to life along this fertile band of Mississippi River flood plain. The citizens of Nouvelle Chartres, Kaskaskia, St. Philippe, and Prairie du Rocher farmed corn, wheat, oats, and barley—enough to supply the far northern colonies of Quebec and Montreal and the sultry southern colony of Louisiana. Here was the breadbasket for all of New France!

The fleur-de-lis flew over French Illinois from the late 1600s until the area was forfeited to the British at the end of the French and Indian War in 1763. The British Union Jack flew over the disgruntled French citizenry until 1778, when Kaskaskia and Prairie du Rocher embraced American Colonel George Rogers Clark and his Virginia "Long Knives." The Commonwealth of Virginia absorbed the new "Illinois Territory" until ceding its holdings to the Continental Congress in 1787. The Northwest Territory (including present-day Ohio, Indiana, Michigan, Wisconsin and part of Minnesota) was established with General Arthur St. Clair as governor. In 1790 St. Clair assigned Cahokia and Kaskaskia to share civil government of the newly designated St. Clair County.

In October of 1795, the southern half of St. Clair County became Randolph County, with old Kaskaskia as its seat of government. Kaskaskia (now located on the Missouri shore, northwest of Chester), became the first Illinois capital in 1818. In 1820 the capital was moved to Vandalia, some 90 miles northeast along the Kaskaskia River. Today Chester is the county seat of Randolph County.

Prairie du Rocher, Illinois
Population 602

Prairie du Rocher may seem a little bit down at the heels—but that may be forgiven when you realize that it recently celebrated its 275th birthday!

Settled in 1722, Prairie du Rocher claims the title of oldest town in Illinois. Cahokia and other villages may in fact be older by 10 to 25 years, but they were started as forts, trading posts or missions rather than towns. The vertical log construction of the new Village Hall and the post office along Illinois Route 155 (Henry Street) is a reminder of traditional French-style construction. Many historic French homes in the valley have been disguised by remodeling and the addition of modern siding. Just for fun, learn to distinguish the distinctive enclosed galleries and peaked rooflines of remodeled colonial homes!

An Historical Note: The more things change ...

In 1766 Captain Philip Pitman visited the Mississippi River on behalf of the English government. In 1770, his book on the "Present State of the European Settlements on the Mississippi" was published in London. It is interesting to do a "then and now" comparison. About Prairie du Rocher, he wrote:

> *About fourteen miles from Cascasquia [Kaskaskia]. A small village of twenty-two dwelling houses inhabited by as many families. The inhabitants are very industrious, and raise a great deal of corn and every kind of stock. The village is two miles from Fort Chartres [this was Little Village, a mile or more nearer than the present Prairie du*

Rocher]. It takes its name from its situation, being built under a rock that runs parallel with the river, at a league distant, for forty miles up."

WHAT TO SEE IN PRAIRIE DU ROCHER

La Maison Creole (The Creole House) ⊨

On Market Street. Open by appointment, 618-282-2245.
An excellent example of French Colonial architecture. Built about 1800, it is operated by the Randolph County Historical Society.

La Maison du Rocher Country Inn (The House of Rock)

Duclos and Main Streets, 618-284-3463. Restaurant, B&B, and gift shop. Closed Mondays.
Built in 1885—partially with stones scavenged from the ruins of the original Fort de Chartres.

St. Joseph Catholic Church ⊨

Duclos and Main Streets.
St. Joseph Church celebrated its 275th anniversary in 1996. The congregation is the second oldest in the state and preserves the French parish registers and communion vessels from the church of Ste. Anne, once located just outside the walls of Fort de Chartres. The congregation treasures several gifts from Louis XV, the King of France during the 1700s.

Historic St. Joseph's Cemetery

From the church, follow Middle Street and Chartrand a few blocks across an unguarded railroad track to the cemetery.
A marker points out the original location of the church. The old village surrounded the church cemetery before drifting toward the bluffs to avoid flooding. The cemetery includes the graves of many of the French Colonial District's earliest pioneer settlers, which were moved from the cemetery at Ste. Anne's. Look for the grave of Fran-

cis Saucier, the engineer charged with the building of Fort de Chartres.

SPECIAL EVENTS IN PRAIRIE DU ROCHER

January, first or second Saturday: *Costume Ball* .

September: *Apple Fete & County Fair*, Creole House, 618-282-2245.

☼

Leave Prairie du Rocher via Henry Street. Follow Illinois Hwy. 155 to Fort de Chartres, four miles to the west.

While crossing the broad prairie to Fort de Chartres, note floodwalls where the road intersects with earthen levees. You may see deteriorating sandbags that remain after having served recent flood duty. Farmers have long lived in the middle of this great flood plain because before the 1850s the damaging floods we see today seldom occurred. Most buildings were built on only a small rise in the land—perhaps upon an Indian mound. Waters then were unrestrained by levees and floodwalls, and the vast northern wetlands were still intact, so even the highest floods meant only a foot of water over the fields for perhaps a day or two.

In contrast, the flood of 1993 was devastating; the river was attic-high on two-story farmhouses in the flatlands. Many long-time farmers blame severe flooding today on the destruction of wetlands to the north.

Fort de Chartres

National Historic Landmark, Prairie du Rocher, Illinois 62277, 618-284-7230. Open 8 a.m. to 5 p.m. Closed Thanksgiving, Christmas and New Year's Day.

Somehow I wasn't prepared for the great limestone fortress that suddenly loomed up in the center of this

INSIGHT

Prairie du Rocher and the Flood of 1993

During dinner at Lisa's Restaurant, Dave Doiron visited with us from a neighboring table about the flood in 1993. The first crest that summer was on August 1. When the levee broke at Columbia, about 25 miles north, waters raced south to flood Valmeyer within six hours. The watery avalanche reached Prairie du Rocher 12 hours later, having methodically washed away much of Valmeyer, Harrisonville, Fults, and Boxtown (Kidd). The river valley drops approximately one foot per mile, so the churning water picked up speed and depth with every mile.

The folks in Prairie du Rocher watched the flood waters rise six inches per hour in the fields. To protect the town, they needed to add three feet to the creek or 'flank' levee, which runs east and west to protect against water coming from the north. They didn't think the levee would hold.

"Blow the river dike!" locals urged the Army Corps of Engineers. Townspeople believed that flooding resulting from a break in the north/south dike along the river (the 20-mile primary dike) would result in less damage to the flank levee as the water would flow in at the same level and with less velocity. As the new flood waters spread north across the fields it could help to absorb the energy of the flood pouring down from the north. A down side, the Corps argued, was that dynamiting the levee might cause the whole structure to collapse.

"We ended up dynamiting *and* using a crane to gouge out a 1000-foot-wide break," Dave explained. "The night before the crest of the northern flood was expected, we were still piling rock and dirt on top of the creek levee. I asked the dikeman what it would take to hold back the oncoming water. He told me glumly that it would take a miracle."

"When we woke up the next day," Dave continued, "the levee had held—thanks to the river water buffer we had fought for. The same day, water levels started to recede."

There was more water in store for the floodplain that year. A second flood crest occurred in October, with high winds and white-capped waves causing more damage to the weakened levees than did the original crest.

broad, silent prairie! Thick walls of white limestone and a heavy iron gate radiated "officialdom," and I unconsciously sat a little straighter in the car. First built of upright logs in 1720, Fort de Chartres was rebuilt in 1753-56 of native stone quarried from the nearby bluffs, making it one of the strongest forts in North America. With the Treaty of Paris in 1763, France ceded the greater portion of her North American possessions to Great Britain, and Fort de Chartres was the last fort the French surrendered. It was abandoned and destroyed in 1772.

Captain Pitman wrote of Fort de Chartres in 1770:

> *The fort is an irregular quadrangle: the sides of the exterior polygon are 490 feet. It is built of stone, and plastered over, and designed as a defense only against the Indians. The walls are two feet two inches thick. The moat was never finished. The buildings within the walls are a commandant's and commissary's house, the magazine of stores, corps de garde, and two barracks. Also a powder magazine, a bake house, a prison with four dungeons and two upper rooms. In the year 1764, there were about forty families in the village near the fort. In the following year, when the English took possession of the country, the French abandoned their houses and settled in the villages on the west side of the Mississippi, choosing to continue under the French government.*

The present fort was reconstructed from the foundations of the ruins, its design based on other forts built by the same engineer, Francis Saucier. Most of the work (building the museum office, the north gate, and the guard house) was done in the 1930s as a CCC project. Only the powder magazine, the oldest stone building in Illinois, is considered to be original. It dates from 1755.

Today Fort de Chartres is the only French fort reconstruction in the United States. Jim Duvall, a guide and avid 1750s reenacter at the fort, showed us water marks from the flood of 1993 that are 13.2 feet high on the narrow portion of the fireplace chimney in the main museum display room. The fort was closed for a year and a half for cleanup after the flood.

HISTORY OF THE FORT

It is believed that two divisions, totaling 135 soldiers, were housed at the fort, as well as the Commandant and officers. The large beds in the guardrooms were designed to accommodate eleven men sleeping head to toe. If the beds look too short for this, remember that most French soldiers were between 4'11" and 5'3" tall.

Several villages encircled the early fort, including Nouvelle Chartres, St. Philippe, and Prairie du Rocher. Civilians farmed corn, wheat, barley, oats and vegetables in the

Plan of the present day Fort.

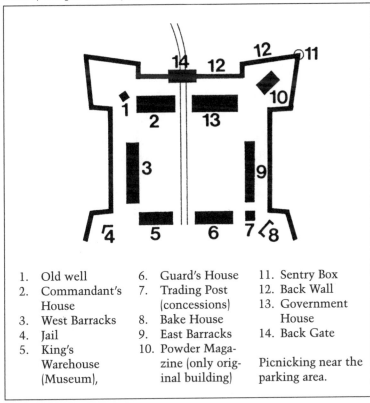

1. Old well	6. Guard's House	11. Sentry Box
2. Commandant's House	7. Trading Post (concessions)	12. Back Wall
3. West Barracks	8. Bake House	13. Government House
4. Jail	9. East Barracks	14. Back Gate
5. King's Warehouse (Museum),	10. Powder Magazine (only original building)	Picnicking near the parking area.

81

Reenacters converge on Fort de Chartres the first weekend in June.

fertile fields. (In the 1740s, 600,000 pounds of wheat per year were shipped from here to New Orleans!) It was these fertile fields that the French forts were built to protect.

THE ST. LOUIS CONNECTION

In 1763, Pierre Laclède, with his paramour, a Mrs. Chouteau, and their 13-year-old son, August, bought a farmhouse outside the fort's gate in Nouvelle Chartres. Four months later, he sold the farm and in 1764 took his family and all his trading supplies and moved north to Cahokia to look for a site for a trading post. He crossed the Mississippi River at Cahokia and chose a site on the west bank.

Laclède offered free land to people from the French district who wanted to settle around his trading post. As the Treaty of Paris had made all of the east bank a territory of Great Britain, many of the French flocked to this new French settlement. The new settlement was originally called San Carlos (a nod to the Spanish government), and in 1780 was renamed as St. Louis.

INSIGHT

A Tale from the Old Fort

Dishonesty in the French community was sorely punished, as illustrated by a story guide Jim Duvall culled from fort records archived in New Orleans. A soldier from the fort was to be hanged for stealing six chickens from a local farmer. He appealed to the Superior Court in New Orleans and was offered a reprieve—provided that he was branded with the letter "V" for *voleur* or thief, that he be whipped in a public pillory, and then be sentenced to spend the rest of his life as a galley slave, rowing one of the King's ships. All for stealing six chickens!

SPECIAL EVENTS AT FORT DE CHARTRES

New Year's Eve: *La Guiannee Singers* at the Fort.

June, first weekend: *Fort de Chartres Summer Rendezvous.* A huge rendezvous recreates the crafts and contests of the early settlers. Tens of thousands of visitors wander among buckskinners and blanket traders offering wares similar to what might have been found in the 1750s. Many 18th-century military groups are represented at the gathering, including the French Village Militia Men, the Royal Highland Regiment, and the French marines. No camping facilities. Call 618-284-7230 for more information.

——————— ✺ ———————

From Fort de Chartres, continue south along Bluff Road to Modoc. The road west from Modoc leads to the Ste. Genevieve-Modoc Ferry and the Missouri shore. The Modoc Rock Shelter is two miles south of Prairie du Rocher on the Bluff Road. It is signed, but is easy to miss. Watch your odometer!

Modoc, Illinois

Population 50

The settlement at Modoc is clustered just under the 100-foot-high rocky bluffs that border scenic Bluff Road. There are no amenities in Modoc, but if you arrive in late spring, you'll admire the brilliant purple lilacs found throughout the district. Many of the first slips were brought over by French settlers just after 1700!

According to *Indian Place Names in Illinois*, published by the Illinois State Historical Society, *modoc* is the Klamath and Modoc Indian word for "south" or "southern." The Modoc Indians themselves live in southern Oregon and northern California. The Modoc tribe became famous when they held off United States troops for months while resisting transfer to reservations in 1872-1873. Why the village name changed from Brewerville to Modoc in 1882 is still unclear.

WHAT TO SEE IN THE MODOC AREA

Modoc Rock Shelter

Since the early 1950s, archeologists have been excavating sediment at the base of the limestone bluff at Modoc. The debris at the base of the bluff has provided an archeological record of human occupation that spans more than 6000 years. Radiocarbon dating of samples found at the bluff date from 4000 to 10,000 years old.

The most significant artifacts span what is known as the Archaic Period, which occurred prior to widespread use of pottery or the adoption of agriculture. In 1984, archeologists from the Illinois State Museum found impressions of a knotted fiber mat in fire-hardened silt nearly 25 feet below the surface. In addition, there were beads made from the shells of marine snails, indicating that even these primitive Indians carried trade items as far as 500 miles from their camping site. During the course of the excavating, scientists have been able to document changes in eating habits of the native Indians, changes in the course of the Mississippi River and changes in climate.

Bluffs and rocky overhangs along Bluff Road are truly beautiful. Occasionally homes and many old sheds and barns seem to shelter under any available rock overhang in an effort to keep buildings and animals cool in the summer and warmer in the winter. It is not hard to imagine early native clans sheltering in much the same way!

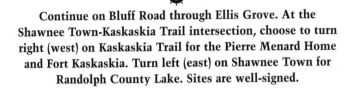

Continue on Bluff Road through Ellis Grove. At the Shawnee Town-Kaskaskia Trail intersection, choose to turn right (west) on Kaskaskia Trail for the Pierre Menard Home and Fort Kaskaskia. Turn left (east) on Shawnee Town for Randolph County Lake. Sites are well-signed.

Ellis Grove, Illinois
Population 353

A junction here rejoins Illinois Hwy 3, the "high road," which is officially Illinois' Great River Road. Deep valleys and rolling hills hide hollows and swampland. We visited the area in early April and enjoyed the deep spring greens after leaving snowflakes the week before in Wisconsin!

WHAT TO SEE IN THE ELLIS GROVE AREA

Randolph County Lake

Located just off the Shawneetown Trail, the lake offers nearly 900 acres of recreation area. Excellent camping, fishing, picnicking, hiking, boat rentals, and bait. Equestrian trails.

Pierre Menard Home State Historic Site

An official site on the George Rogers Clark Historic Trail. Open 9 a.m. to 5 p.m., 618-859-3031.

The Pierre Menard Home is another important leg in the reconstruction of French history in southwestern Illi-

nois. The home was built in 1800 by the first lieutenant governor of Illinois and is considered to be the finest example of French Colonial architecture in the Midwest.

Pierre Menard and his historic home.

Fort Kaskaskia State Historic Site

Located just up the hill from the Pierre Menard Home, this is a major Illinois state historic site with extensive picnicking and camping. Metal detectors are not allowed in the park. Playground, toilets, and RV dump station. 618-859-3741.

Much of the park is situated on a limestone bluff that is riddled with caves. As water runs through the ceiling of a limestone cave, it carries away minerals, weakening the ceiling. Sometimes the ceiling will collapse into the cave, causing the earth above it to sink and form a steep-sided depression. This is called a *sinkhole*. One such sinkhole is clearly visible just to the left at the top of the park road before the fort foundations appear. (See *karst topography on page 43.*)

INSIGHT

Pierre Menard, Frontiersman/Statesman

I thought it interesting to learn about a young Frenchman who made his fortune in the settlement of Kaskaskia and rose to lieutenant governor of the new state of Illinois.

Pierre Menard was born near Montreal in 1766. He left home at the age of 15 to sign on as a *voyageur*. Pierre had friends in Vincennes, Illinois, where he became a clerk for François Vigo in 1786. There he was convinced to join a party traveling with Arthur St. Clair to set up a government in the Northwest Territories. He arrived in Kaskaskia with St. Clair and settled there in1790. He married Therese Godin in 1792 and they had four children. Therese died in 1804 and Menard remarried, to Angelique Saucier, the daughter of the engineer at Fort de Chartres. With Angelique he had eight more children.

Besides being a storekeeper and trader, Menard operated a ferry at Kaskaskia across the Kaskaskia River and became a large property owner in several counties.

Menard's business alliances were legion. He was a business partner of merchants Louis Bolduc and François Valle of Ste. Genevieve as well as of Pierre Chouteau in St. Louis. In 1801, the Spanish granted Menard the privileges of trading for peltry with the Indians on the Saline River, below Ste. Genevieve, and making salt there. Menard and Valle joined forces with the arrival of the first steamboat in 1817. He invested in the first trading expedition of Manuel Lisa (the first fur trader on the upper Missouri) during the winter of 1806-1807 and accompanied Lisa on a journey up the Missouri from June 1809 to July 1810.

Menard was also a subagent for the United States Indian Department from 1813 to 1838. During that time he directed the Mississippi River crossings of emigrating Indians. He was elected Lt. Governor of Illinois and served with Governor Shadrach Bond from 1818 to 1822.

Menard died on June 13, 1844. The Menard family plot is located at Fort Kaskaskia. Menard County was named for him in 1839, and a statue of him placed on the Capitol grounds at Springfield in 1888.

Today as you walk up the steps to the fort site, the surrounding earth is lumpy from the foundations of the old fort built in 1759—outer walls of upright logs and the remains of a dry moat which surrounded the fort. The fort overlooks Kaskaskia Island; the original town would have been at the north end of the island below (in the vicinity of Kaskaskia River Lock & Dam). Ste. Genevieve sits at the base of the bluffs far to the west where the original channel of the Mississippi River once flowed. Most of the wetland below is backwater areas or sloughs of the Mississippi and Kaskaskia rivers. Walk to the stone shelter above the Obelisk to see the actual mouth of the Kaskaskia River.

The Obelisk, near the Garrison Hill Cemetery by the park office parking area, was erected as a memorial to Illinois pioneers in 1893. A partial listing of pioneer names is available at the site office. The gravestones near the Obelisk were moved in 1881 from the old cemetery in Kaskaskia to preserve them from erosion after the Mississippi River cut through the narrow peninsula of land and made the island now visible below.

SPECIAL EVENTS IN THE ELLIS GROVE AREA

January, first Sunday: *Celebration at Pierre Menard Home,* 618-284-7230 or 618-859-3031.

September, fourth weekend: *Fort Kaskaskia Traditional Music Festival,* Ellis Grove.

December: *Christmas Open House and Candlelight Tour* at Pierre Menard Home, 618-859-3031.

———————————— ⚙ ————————————

Return to Hwy. 3 and continue south to Chester. To visit what remains of present-day Kaskaskia, on Kaskaskia Island, cross the Chester Bridge over the Mississippi onto Missouri Hwy. 51. Turn north on Cty. H. Travel through rolling countryside to U.S. Hwy. 61 and turn north toward St. Mary's, Missouri. Follow the signs to Kaskaskia Island.

Kaskaskia, Illinois
Population 18

K askaskia Island is the only populated Illinois territory located west of the Mississippi.

WHAT TO SEE ON KASKASKIA ISLAND

Kaskaskia Bell ❼   ⊤▪

Open 8 a.m. to 5 p.m., 618-859-3741.

The main historic attraction on the nearly unpopulated island is the 650-pound Kaskaskia Bell, given to the Church of the Immaculate Conception in 1741 by King Louis XV. This bell was rung by Father Pierre Gibaut, the "Patriot Priest," on July 4, 1778, to celebrate the capture of Kaskaskia by Colonel George Rogers Clark. Officially designated as the "Liberty Bell of the West," it is older than the Liberty Bell in Philadelphia. It is inscribed "For the church of Illinois—by the gift of the King."

The Church of the Immaculate Conception

This is the same church made famous by photos taken during the flood of 1993, when only the top one third of the spire poked above a slurry of brown water. A sign outside says the congregation was founded by Father James Marquette in 1675, though the first home of the congregation was far to the northeast, in central Illinois.

When I visited in 1996 the church appeared to have been bombed—bare, shattered walls, plaster falling off to reveal laths, bubbled paint, stained glass windows gone altogether. Yet chatting merrily around a huge quilt project were 13 church women creating a quilt to raffle off for restoration funds.

The ladies told me that the flood was unexpected here. The levees are 50 feet high and the crest was to be only 47 feet. But *sandboils* (weak spots where water begins percolating up through the compacted soil of the levee) caused enough damage that a hollow formed and the levee collapsed. People and equipment had to be evacuated quickly from the island. Some of the church's 300-year-old treasures had been stored for safety in the choir loft, including the hand-carved altar and pulpit, but floating pews and other furnishings smashed out the stained glass windows and floated on down the river.

The congregation is determined to maintain its church, although the Diocese of Belleville originally seemed equally as determined to close the water-damaged building. Threatened with closure, the congregation has worked determinedly to restore and staff the church. The major fund raiser is the annual church picnic on the Sunday before Labor Day in September. Several books for sale in the entryway document the efforts of area residents to protect the entire French Colonial District from devastating floods.

SPECIAL EVENTS ON KASKASKIA ISLAND

July 4: *Kaskaskia Island Patriotic Program.* Three-day event with fireworks. 618-859-3741.

Women of Kaskaskia Island's Church of the Immaculate Conception raise money to restore flood damage by raffling quilts.

INSIGHT

A Brief History of the Old Village of Kaskaskia and How It Came to an End

It is easy to stand at the bluff at the Fort Kaskaskia State Historic Site and imagine oneself transported back to the late 1700s. The first settlement of what became Kaskaskia began in 1703 at the confluence of the Kaskaskia and Mississippi Rivers. It was to be a trading center and mission to the local natives of the Illini Confederation. Constant conflict between France and England prompted the local citizens to request the presence of a fort. A fort started in 1734 was never completed. A second fort was completed in 1736 but was never garrisoned by French troops. After 1764 and the Treaty of Paris, citizens destroyed the fort to keep the British from occupying it. Captain Pitman writes in 1766:

> *The village of Notre Dame de Cascasquias is by far the most considerable settlement in the country of the Illinois Indians. Sixty-five families reside in the village, in addition to merchants and slaves. The church, the Jesuits' House and some other houses in the village are built of stone and make a very good appearance. Canoe convoys carry furs and farm produce from Cascasquias and Kaoquias to Canada and New Orleans.*
>
> *The fort, which was burnt down in October 1766, stood on the summit of a high rock opposite the village and on the opposite side of the river. It was an oblong quadrangle, of which the extreme polygon measured 290 by 251 feet. It was built of very thick square timber, and dove-tailed at the angles. An officer and twenty soldiers were quartered in the village under the direction of the Commandant at Fort de Chartres.*

After the 1850s, the Mississippi River began nibbling away at the peninsula of land on which the city sat. Finally, in April of 1881, a flood and ice jam allowed the Mississippi River to break through and pour along the narrow course of the Kaskaskia. The town was located at the north end of the peninsula and it wasn't long before the entire town was simply gobbled up by the rampaging waters of the Mississippi.

Continued ...

Herb Meyer, an historian of the French Colonial Period, described the "end" of French Kaskaskia in this way:

By 1881, the year the Mississippi first broke through the narrows into the Kaskaskia (Okaw) River, the city was already 180 years old. For the past 15 years, the river had been nibbling away at the narrows—a strip of land separating it from the Kaskaskia River—creeping ever eastward, about 1½ miles above Kaskaskia. By 1879 only ½ mile separated the two rivers.

For several years up to 1880, the Mississippi River Commission had held the Mississippi at bay with piers and other structures, but unusually heavy snow fell in Minnesota and Wisconsin during the winter of '80-81. Severely cold temperatures allowed ice to freeze to one and two feet. When the river suddenly rose eight feet on February 10, 1881, the ice gorged through the protective barriers, allowing water to flow behind the structures and cause extensive damage. By April, the distance between the two rivers was about 400-500 feet. When a strong northwesterly sprang up over the rising river, "great waves" ran across the surface of the Narrows, eating away the soft, sandy west bank of the Kaskaskia. On April 18, the Narrows broke entirely away and the Mississippi, some eight feet higher than the Kaskaskia, began a great rush both up and down the smaller river channel. In the darkness, the chasm widened from feet to yards in a matter of minutes.

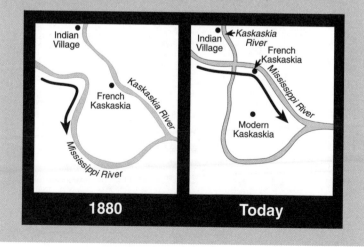

Spectators who came from throughout the region at dawn watched as water surged with such force that great chunks of soil collapsed into the flood. Trees began to fall, "strips of land a half acre or more caved off into the water" with a noise "like distant thunder or the booming of cannon." Whole groves of trees were swept into the muddy channel of the two combined rivers.

Within a week after the breakthrough, the cut across the Narrows was big enough for a steamboat to pass through. Through the next ten years the Mississippi flowed on either side of the new island, gradually eating away at the soft west bank where Kaskaskia sat. By the late 1890s the entire main channel of the Mississippi was able to go through the Kaskaskia channel. For another decade, the Mississippi nibbled at the old city. Each year some part of the town along its north and east sides would slip into the widening river until the river had reached the building in the center of town which had once been the seat of government of the new state of Illinois. First its large double chimney fell into the river, and the rest soon followed. By 1917 virtually all the town had been taken.

The village of New Kaskaskia was rebuilt in the center of the island. The old Randolph County Courthouse and the large brick church built in 1843 were torn down and reassembled on the new site. This new site, too, is subject to occasionally devastating floods.

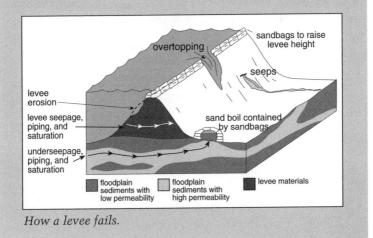

How a levee fails.

—— O ——

Return to Chester (9 miles) via State Hwy. 61,
Cty. H and Hwy. 51.

Chester, Illinois
Population 8204

Enjoy a pleasant rural drive from Kaskaskia to Chester, through rolling hills, pecan groves, peach and apple orchards, and, in April, dogwood, redbud and other flowering bushes. Near Chester, the roads are marked with warnings not to pick up hitchhikers. The Menard Maximum Security Prison, established in 1877, is built on the bluffs, and the prison population and that of the nearby Chester Mental Health Center total between 2500 and 3000—nearly one third of the town's population. The Gilster Mary-Lee Corporation is the major private employer in the area. Con-Agra Flour Mills got its start in Chester when Nathan Cole founded the Cole Milling Company in 1837.

South of Chester, the Great River Road dips abruptly down to river level and offers one of the few opportunities to drive a scenic nine miles right along the Mississippi without a levee blocking the view. Chester itself is built on the bluff, however, so visit here first and then continue along the Great River Road to Rockwood. Illinois Highway 150 is also called State Street and is the main street in town. Bridge Approach Road leads to the bridge to Missouri and Missouri Highway 51. This is also the route to Kaskaskia Island.

A BRIEF HISTORY OF CHESTER
Local history suggests that the town was established in 1829 and named for Chester, England. Samuel Smith established the first home, ran a ferry and a mill, and hired out as a surveyor. Castor oil was produced from locally grown

beans and exchanged for beeswax, deerskins, hides, and all types of produce. At one time a thousand coonskins costing 25 cents each were shipped from Chester to Liverpool, England, and sold for $1 a skin.

FOOD AND ACCOMMODATIONS IN CHESTER

For accommodations, call **Reids' Inn Best Western Hotel,** 618-826-3034. **Reids' Harvest House Smorgasbord** attracts visitors from throughout southern Illinois and neighboring states. **The Old Landmark Inn** overlooking the Mississippi River is a good choice for steak.

For Randolph County tourism information, contact the Tourism Committee, P.O. Box 332, Chester, IL 62233. 618-826-5000. ext. 221, or the Southwestern Illinois Tourism Bureau, 10950 Lincoln Trail, Fairview Heights, IL 62208. 1-800-442-1488.

WHAT TO SEE IN CHESTER

Popeye the Sailor Man Bronze Statue

*At the Chester bridge to Missouri in **Elzie Segar Memorial Park**.*

An 8-foot statue of Popeye commemorates Elzie Crisler Segar, the creator of the jut-jawed Popeye. Segar was born in Chester in 1894 and died in California in 1938.

Spinach Can Collectibles

State Street, 618-826-4567.

The only Popeye Store and Museum in the nation, this is also home to the Popeye Fan Club, comprised of 650 members from as far away as Australia—mostly collectors of Popeye memorabilia. Visitors will find Popeye T-Shirts, comic books, sketches, and more.

Visit the park at **Chester Square** next door to the Popeye Museum: 1890s-style gazebo and a view of the Popeye Mural.

Randolph County Courthouse
& Museum & Archives Buildings ⊩

1 Taylor Street, 618-826-2510. Museum open weekday afternoons in season.

Visit the fifth floor observatory in the modern Randolph County Courthouse, which overlooks the Mississippi River and the Missouri shore. The rotunda, five stories overhead, is accessible by two large circular staircases that wind to the observation deck 353 feet above the river. The Missouri hills visible from this vantage point are the foothills of the Ozarks. If you don't feel like climbing five stories, there is an elevator, or you can just park and sit on the park bench near the stone courthouse Annex. The river view is excellent.

This modern building is the third structure to serve as Randolph County Courthouse. The original was in Kaskaskia; the second, built in Chester after disastrous flooding in 1844, has since been demolished. The squatty stone Courthouse Annex built in 1864 now houses museum of local history from French Colonial to modern days.

The Gordon "Bud" Cohen Mansion ⊩

Along the river bluffs on Harrison Street. The city operates the benefactor's restored home with a river overlook. Open weekend afternoons in season.

Mary's River Covered Bridge ⊩

On the Old Plank Road. Follow Highway 150 east about five miles from downtown Chester.

The covered bridge is about 150 feet long and is more than 100 years old. The Plank Road connected Chester with Steeleville and was planked to allow travel during muddy spring conditions. The original Plank Road ran roughly parallel to Highway 150.

Governor Shadrach Bond State Memorial ⊩

In Evergreen Cemetery along Illinois Route 3.

The memorial commemorates the territory's first representative and Illinois' first state governor. Raised as a farmer near Baltimore, Maryland, Bond immigrated to the Illinois Territory in 1794 and farmed first near Chester and then moved to a farm in Kaskaskia in 1814. The memorial marks the final resting place of Bond and his wife.

Turkey Bluffs State Fish & Wildlife Area

South of Chester on Hwy 3. Scenic overlook on highway, picnicking, hiking, horse trails, river overlooks.

The Chester Country Club

Offers nine holes of golf to the public.

Cole Memorial Park & Pool

Public swimming between Memorial Day and Labor Day for a small fee. The name commemorates Nathan Cole, who emigrated to the Illinois Territory in 1837. Cole's Milling Co. eventually grew into Con-Agra.

SPECIAL EVENTS IN CHESTER

September, weekend after Labor Day: *Popeye Picnic,* 618-826-2326 or 826-4567.

December, first weekend: *Christmas on the River,* 618-826-2326.

Continue on Hwy. 3 to Rockwood, 4 miles south of Turkey Bluffs overlook.

After Rockwood, Highway 3 leaves the river and once again threads its way through broad, flat fields. The river winds its way back toward Missouri.

Jackson & Union
Counties, Illinois

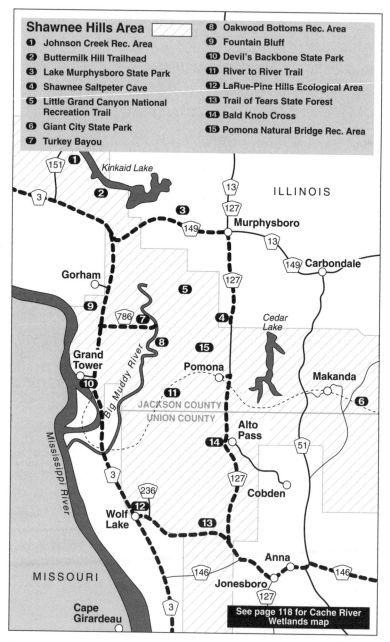

Shawnee Hills Area

1. Johnson Creek Rec. Area
2. Buttermilk Hill Trailhead
3. Lake Murphysboro State Park
4. Shawnee Saltpeter Cave
5. Little Grand Canyon National Recreation Trail
6. Giant City State Park
7. Turkey Bayou
8. Oakwood Bottoms Rec. Area
9. Fountain Bluff
10. Devil's Backbone State Park
11. River to River Trail
12. LaRue-Pine Hills Ecological Area
13. Trail of Tears State Forest
14. Bald Knob Cross
15. Pomona Natural Bridge Rec. Area

Kinkaid Lake

ILLINOIS

Murphysboro

Carbondale

Gorham

Cedar Lake

Grand Tower

Pomona

Makanda

JACKSON COUNTY
UNION COUNTY

Big Muddy River

Mississippi River

Alto Pass

Cobden

Wolf Lake

Anna

MISSOURI

Jonesboro

Cape Girardeau

See page 118 for Cache River Wetlands map

7

Jackson, Union, & Pulaski Counties, Illinois

The placid valley drive along Illinois Route 3 in northern Jackson County disguises a unique environmental phenomenon. Hidden inland of the limestone bluffs lining the Great River Road, the northern extremity of the Illinois Ozarks blends seamlessly into the unglaciated Shawnee Hills of southern Illinois. Along the Cache River basin in the southernmost part of the state, coastal plain swamps are remnants of the days when an ancient shallow sea abutted the limestone escarpment just south of Carbondale and Murphysboro.

Today, the Shawnee National Forest, Trail of Tears State Forest and the Cypress Creek National Wildlife Refuge in the Cache River basin offer visitors many opportunities to explore the five distinct ecological and biological divisions found in this compact area. Fall foliage throughout southern Illinois is outstanding. Maple, gum and dogwood produce brilliant reds. Beech trees glow yellow and oaks are scarlet-brown.

Near Cache, *bald cypress*, a soft cedar-like tree, appears for the first time. Cypress are swamp-loving trees that bring a true southern flavor to the river road. They are deciduous—a relative of the California redwood and the northern tamarack—and one of the few needle-bearing trees that lose their leaves. The *tupelo gum* is the most common

INSIGHT

Ecological Divisions of Southwestern Illinois

According to the National Forest Service, the unique diversity of plant and animal life in Southern Illinois is directly related to the diverse ecological divisions that fit compactly into this largely unglaciated tip between the Ohio and Mississippi Rivers. Watch for variations in rock outcroppings, topography, and tree cover to signal changing divisions as you travel.

The Lower Mississippi River Bottomlands Division stretches along the river and its floodplain from Alton, Illinois to the Thebes Gorge. The northern section (the American Bottom) originally contained prairies, marshes, and forests. The southern section was densely forested and contained a greater number of tree species than the forests of the Upper Mississippi River, including some southern lowland species. Northern plant communities are comprised of moisture-loving species generally found on north-facing slopes.

Prairie communities in isolated hill prairies and limestone glades are most common in the limestone bluffs of the **Illinois Ozarks Division,** which stretches from northern Monroe County southward. Forested areas contain butternut, black walnut and other hickories, as well as sugar maple, basswood, oaks, and the early coloring tulip tree. White oak, sycamore, American elm, river birch, cherry and cottonwood are found in the floodplain area.

The **Shawnee Hills Division** stretches from Fountain Bluff on the Mississippi River to the Shawneetown Hills near the mouth of the Wabash River. This unglaciated hill country is characterized by a high escarpment of Pennsylvanian sandstone cliffs in its northern section and a series of lower limestone hills at its lower reaches. The topography here is very rugged, with many bluffs, ravines, and canyons eroded by streams. Plant species found here are generally hardy, fire-loving species such as poplar, hickory, and oak.

Bald cypress and tupelo-gum swamps are a unique feature of the **Coastal Plain Division** which begins at Olive Branch

Continued on next page

water-loving deciduous tree in the wet bottomland of the Mississippi and Ohio rivers. *Pumpkin ash* and *water elm* are also found in the Cache River basin.

More than one million Canada geese and snow geese spend the winter in southern Illinois, and much of the wetland is professionally managed for environmental and hunting use. Many camping, fishing, and wildlife viewing areas are accessible from Illinois Route 3. In addition, natural attractions on either side of the Highway 127 south of Murphysboro are noted so that the traveler may take advantage of various state and national preserves and enjoy some of the diverse ecological treasures in southernmost Illinois.

and includes the Cache River Basin. Although unglaciated, the area has been carved by glacial meltwater. Glacial Lake Cache formed in the valleys of the Cache and Ohio rivers during a late stage of glaciation. Bedrock in the area is deeply covered by alluvium: sands, gravels, and clays deposited by water.

Source: Comprehensive Plan for the Illinois Nature Preserves System, John E. Schwegman, principal author.

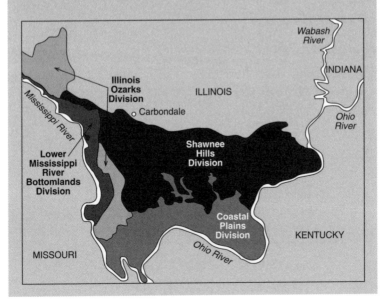

Murphysboro/Carbondale, Illinois

Enter Jackson County on Illinois Hwy. 3 just south of
Rockwood, IL.

RECREATION AREAS NORTH OF THE MURPHYSBORO/CARBONDALE EXIT

Johnson Creek Recreation Area ❶

*5 miles to the north and east of Illinois 3 on Illinois 151. On
Lake Kinkaid, near Ava.*

Johnson Creek Campground

*On the west end of Kinkaid Lake, 618-687-1731. Open mid-May
to September. Picnic tables, flush toilets, boat launch, swimming beach.*

Buttermilk Hill Trail Head,
Buttermilk Hill Beach and Picnic Area ❷

*On Kinkaid Lake, 1½ miles west of the main marina. Accessi-
ble only by boat or a 2.5-mile trail.*

Sharp Rock Falls Campground

*On Highway 151 about 3 miles south of Ava on Kinkaid Lake,
618-763-5511. Open year-round. 20 sites with electricity, water,
sewer. 40 primitive tent sites, flush toilets, picnic tables, playground, snack bar.*

Although the official Great River Road follows Hwy. 3
south to Cairo, several side trips are recommended.
The first is to the Murphysboro/Carbondale area. Go east
on Hwy. 149 to reach Murphysboro.

RECREATION AREAS OFF HIGHWAY 149
BETWEEN HIGHWAY 3 AND MURPHYSBORO

Lake Kinkaid Village Marina and Campground ⛴ ⛺

On Highway 149, follow Kinkaid Lake and Lake Murphysboro signs, 618-687-4914. Water (March-November), electricity, flush toilets, dump station, ski shop. Full service marina.

Big Oak Campground ⛺

Turn north on an access road about two miles west of Murphysboro on Illinois 149 (follow the Kinkaid Lake/Lake Murphysboro sign), 618-684-2867. Open year-round. 54 camp sites, water, electricity, fire pits, picnic tables, dump station. Tent camping at Shady Rest and Waterlily camp areas.

Lake Murphysboro State Park ❸ ⛺

Just west of Murphysboro off Illinois Rt. 149, 618-684-2867. The principal attraction is a man-made lake totaling 145 acres. Fishing, camping.

LODGING IN THE MURPHYSBORO/
CARBONDALE AREA

Lodging is available in Murphysboro and Carbondale. Carbondale is located at the juncture of Illinois Routes 149 and 127. Its name reflects the importance of minerals to the area: salt, coal, fluorspar and tripoli have all been mined in the area. Call 800-526-1500 for information.

The Shawnee National Forest

Murphysboro Ranger Station is a district office of the Shawnee National Forest and can be contacted at 618-658-2111.

The Shawnee National Forest blankets 275,000 acres of deeply pitted, unglaciated land that is notable for its sandstone features and diversity of plant and animal life. The southernmost glacier to lie upon Illinois was the Illinoian Sheet of 125,000 to 500,000 years ago. Its lower edge rested near modern-day Carbondale and Murphysboro. As the glacier receded, meltwater eroded its way through the 300 million-year-old sandstone in what is today's Shawnee National Forest. Some plant species you'll see in the area are relics from the glacial ages.

Fifty-two species of reptiles and 57 species of amphibians inhabit the limestone bluffs or the swampland in which they are steeped. Look for 49 species of mammals, 253 birds and 109 different species of fish! Be observant. Though seldom seen, timber rattlers, copperheads, mud snakes, and cottonmouths inhabit the area.

Amazingly, it is possible to drive along the flat Mississippi River bottomlands on Illinois Route 3 and never know that this scenic region is just six or seven miles inland. Do not be tempted to pass up Inspiration Point or the drive to Bald Knob Cross in Alto Pass! The LaRue-Pine Hills area is another especially lovely place to drive through, though autos are banned each April and October to accommodate the reptile migration to and from wintering grounds in the bluffs.

The Shawnee National Forest includes thirteen developed campgrounds, 135 miles of hiking trails and 1250 miles of scenic forest roads. Plan to visit in the fall or spring months, as this area can be extremely hot and humid for weeks at a time during the summer, and nighttime brings little relief. Hiking, boating, canoeing, birding, fishing and hunting are all available in the forest.

WHAT TO SEE IN THE MURPHYSBORO/ CARBONDALE AREA OF THE SHAWNEE NATIONAL FOREST

Many scenic vistas and interesting villages are tucked away in the hills along Illinois 127 south of Murphysboro and Highway 51 south of Carbondale. Route 127 forms a dividing line between the limestone bluffs of the Ozark Division and the sandstone prevalent in the Shawnee Hills Division of southwest Illinois (see page 101).

Shawnee Saltpeter Cave ❹   𝕏 𝔸

Six miles south of Murphysboro on Route 127. Entry fee.

This is Illinois' largest bluff shelter. It is a natural amphitheater and the site of a privately operated park featuring strange rock formations and a roaring waterfall. This is an excellent family-oriented attraction with picnic tables, nature trails, paddleboats and canoes.

Little Grand Canyon National Recreation Trail ❺   𝕏

Seven miles south of Murphysboro on Illinois 127, 618-687-1731.

This site is well recommended. A 3.6-mile-long trail descends into a deep ravine and then up the opposite bluff, from which the Mississippi River is visible on a clear day. A portion of the trail follows a steep stream bed that may not be accessible to the casual hiker in icy or wet weather. Although the trail is described as "not strenuous," hiking shoes are recommended. Enjoy woodlands, prairies, waterfalls, and cliffs. The ravine encompasses 1,372 acres and is recognized as an area of great plant and animal diversity, with 650 flowering plants and 27 fern species identified.

Visits to the village of Alto Pass, the Bald Knob Cross, and the Pomona Natural Bridge Recreational Area, all located south of Murphysboro, are recommended, but addressed in this guide as side trips out of Trail of Tears State Forest.

Giant City State Park ❻   ▲ 𝕏 𝔸

South of Carbondale and east of Makanda. 618-457-4836. The beautiful park lodge was built in the 1930s and was recently restored. Serves three meals a day and has a swimming pool, gift shop, and lounge. Phone 618-457-4921 for reservations. Picnicking, hiking, RV and tent camping, equestrian camp.

Unusual rock formations of Pennsylvanian bedrock called Pounds sandstone reportedly looked like the streets of a "giant city" to early settlers. Climb the water tower (open to the public) for a grand overlook of the Shawnee Hills.

Cedar Lake

A 1750-acre lake located six miles south of Murphysboro between U.S. 51 and Illinois 127. 10-horsepower limit. Fishing.

Return to Illinois Route 3 and continue south toward Grand Tower.

Grand Tower, Illinois
Population 800

Originally known as Jenkin's Landing, Grand Tower once boasted a shipyard and a population of 4,000. There is a café and a medical center in the town. Today, **Devil's Backbone State Park** in Grand Tower is nicely developed and offers great views of the river and the area's

Tower Rock is visible in the river just off the Missouri shore at Grand Tower. The 60-foot-high landmark, with a top surface of less than an acre, was purchased during Civil War days as a pier for a bridge that was never built. When released to the public by President Ulysses S. Grant, it was called the smallest national park in the nation. There is a lovely spot for viewing the rock near Wittenburg, on Missouri's shore.

landmark rocks. The large red and white Pipeline Bridge dominates the river view. The pipeline, which originally ran under the river, carries natural gas from Texas.

Across the river was the German town of Wittenburg and the picturesque landing site of the Saxony Lutherans, immigrants who eventually founded the Missouri Synod, Lutheran Church. (See page 145 for more information.)

Devil's Bake Oven is a small rock structure almost directly under the Pipeline Bridge. Named for the many small caves along its base, it affords an excellent overlook of Tower Rock. There is an easy hiking trail around the Devil's Bake Oven. A gentleman from the Missouri shore told me that a ferry crossing long available between Wittenburg and Tower Rock was one of the prettiest crossings on the river because of the rock formations. These boat-snagging rocks so harried steamboat pilots that this stretch of river was referred to as "the graveyard."

SPECIAL EVENTS IN GRAND TOWER

June: *Tower Rock Arts and Crafts Festival* on the riverfront. 618-565-8384.

WHAT TO SEE IN THE GRAND TOWER AREA

Turkey Bayou, River Access Site ❼

North of Grand Tower. Turn off Highway 3 onto Forest Road 186 (Johns Spur Road) and then onto Forest Road 786. Access to the Big Muddy River.

Turkey Bayou Campground

Located east of Highway 3 between Gorham and Grand Tower. Look for a sign about two miles south of the Gorham turnoff. From there it's three miles to the campground, 618-687-1731. Open May 1- December 15. Primitive camping only; water may or may not be available. Hunting, hiking, boat launch (located at the Big Muddy Boat Launch, before you reach the campground) The Big Muddy is a popular fishing river and a candidate

Beau Inman, Riverman

Beau Inman grew up in this area when his dad ran the ferry for the Perry Lumber Company, one of the largest lumber companies in the world. Beau lived across the river in Wittenburg and remembers walking across the suspension pipeline bridge on the four-foot wide pipes. There is no catwalk, just a hand-held cable.

River piloting runs deep in this riverman's veins. Beau's granddad, Ellis Truman, and then his dad, Charles Inman, operated the first family ferry at Winfield, Missouri, from 1892 until 1966 when his dad designed the *Miss June* (named for his wife) and started the Tower Rock Ferry at Wittenburg, Missouri.

"I grew up on that boat," Beau recalls. "I started to steer it when I was eight. By the time I turned ten, I had enough hours logged to get my pilot's license. 'Course they didn't give pilot licenses to ten-year-old kids."

When Charles began hauling logs downriver for the East Perry Lumber Company, June Inman took over as the ferry pilot and became only the second woman licensed as a river pilot in the United States.

"I continued to ride the ferry with my mom between Tower Rock and Wittenburg until the pontoon boat in Prairie du Chien, Wisconsin was dismantled. We moved the ferry up there and carried up to 1200 cars a day. Eventually, my dad and brother and I set up ferries at Beardstown on the Illinois River and between Ste. Genevieve and Modoc, Illinois. I met my wife operating the ferry at Cassville, Wisconsin. I've been away from the river for a while now," he mused, "but I'm back to recover my pilot's license."

I recently saw Beau piloting the *Julia Belle Swain* in La Crosse. "I'm a captain now," he beamed, "I got my license back."

for a Wild and Scenic Rivers designation. The riverbed follows a meander of the prehistoric Mississippi that crossed east to follow the limestone bluffs walls.

INSIGHT

Devil's Backbone and the "Lost Hills"

Devil's Backbone and Fountain Bluff are referred to by geographers as "lost hills"—solitary bluffs or ridges running along the river's edge and surrounded by very flat bottomland terrain. The Mississippi has flowed to the east and to the west of these formations, thus cutting each off from its fellow hills. The term "lost hill" comes from the observation that these hills seem to have wandered off from their brethren.

Oakwood Bottoms Recreation Area/ Greentree Reservoir ❽

Six miles south of Murphysboro, 800-526-1500. Bottomland habitat for ducks and migrating waterfowl. An excellent wayside with boardwalk into a forest wetland. Pond and interpretive information.

Fountain Bluff ❾

North of Grand Tower near Route 3, 618-565-8384.
   This rock formation, with a beautiful view of Southern Illinois, is an example of a "lost hill."

Devil's Backbone State Park ❿

At Grand Tower on the Mississippi River, 618-565-2454. Camping March 1 to November 1. Horse trails open year-round. Camping with electricity and water—separate from the horse camp (see below). Picnic tables, grills, flush toilets, showers, playground, concessions.

Devil's Backbone Horse Camp

Grand Tower City Park, 618-565-2497 or 618-565-2237. Two acres fenced for horses. Electric and water hookups.

River to River Trail ⓫

From Grand Tower to Battery Rock on the Ohio River.
   This 146-mile trail is a hiker's and horseback rider's

dream! It is mainly a Shawnee National Forest trail, but it crosses Ferne Clyffe and Giant City State Parks and is considered to pass through some of the most spectacular scenery in the midwest. There are seven other "wilderness" trails throughout the Shawnee National Forest that are available only to hikers and equestrians.

In April, the River to River Relay is held. This is a road race for teams of eight runners for a total distance of 80 miles, from daylight to dusk. Call for information and admission fee, 618-549-6267 or 997-3690.

— ☼ —

Continue south on Illinois 3 to Wolf Lake for a second side trip—to LaRue-Pine Hills Ecological Area, Trail of Tears State Forest, Alto Pass and Jonesboro.

Wolf Lake

WHAT TO SEE IN THE WOLF LAKE AREA

LaRue-Pine Hills Ecological Area, Southern Entrance ⑫

From Wolf Lake, go east on Illinois 13 for .6 mile, then follow the sign north on Forest Road 236. There are pull-offs for observation points and trails along the way. The road is closed each April and October as reptiles and amphibians migrate from the swamps to the fractured limestone and talus slopes where they den up below the frost line.

Upon leaving the cornfields of Illinois 3, we are immediately immersed in the light-dappled shadows of a great canopy of trees that arch over the gravel roadway. The remains of several small sharecropper cabins dot the 8-mile-long roadway. Unfortunately, our road tour ends abruptly when we find the road closed to automobiles—the snakes are migrating.

Inspiration Point

Within the Pine Hills Recreation Area.

Inspiration Point rises 350 feet above the Mississippi River flood plain. The three-quarter-mile walk on Inspiration Point Forest Trail leads along dry and narrow ridges and downward to deep, cool valleys. At the halfway point, the vista at Inspiration Point is exceptional: On the southwest horizon are the Missouri Ozarks; directly below (350 feet) is the LaRue Scenic Area; between the two are the winding river and the rich farms of the Mississippi Valley. At the end of the Forest Road is a T-intersection. Take a left to get to the bottom of the same cliffs—another impressive sight.

Trail of Tears State Forest ⑬   ⚠ 🚶 ⛾

Continue on Illinois 13 east of Wolf Lake and follow the signs, 618-833-4910. Three public hiking trails leave from the main trailhead. In season, there is public hunting of deer, turkey, quail and squirrel. Picnic tables, shelters, and primitive camping at the trailhead. The 18 miles of equestrian trails are considered to be among the best in the state. Auto access to scenic ridgetop drives.

Trail of Tears State Forest is intended to be a fairly primitive wilderness preserve. It has not been logged in 80 years, so look for large white, red, and black oaks, dogwood, sweet gum, and cypress trees. White oak is the Illinois state tree. The gravel auto trails in the forest are very scenic and fine for driving, though they're fairly adventuresome, often following narrow ridgetops above steep ravines. Never glaciated, this is considered to be some of the most rugged terrain in the state. The site superintendent explained the diverse geology of the area in this way: The flatlands are alluvial plains—sand, gravel and clay deposited by glacial meltwater and river floods. Limestone was formed by ancient reefs; sandstone by the river systems. Layers of shale were left from massive swamps. Coal formations in the Illinois Basin (northern portions of the Shawnee Hills area) were created when the swamps decomposed.

Stonework creek walls and shelters scattered throughout the forest were built by Franklin D. Roosevelt's Civilian Conservation Corps (CCC) and are currently being restored. Nearly 60 years old, many of the stone walls were built without mortar.

On my visit, I spotted a three-foot-long timber rattler near a log on the edge of our path, not twenty feet from the car. It puffed itself up with air and then flattened itself to look as large as possible. Andy, the site superintendent, was as thrilled as I was to spot it.  He considers the timber rattler a very misunderstood snake. In the six years he's been at Trail of Tears, he's never heard of anyone being bitten by a venomous snake—and there are several species in the area.

The timber rattler, Andy told us, is a protected species, in part because it reproduces so slowly. The females don't start reproducing until they are about five years old and then produce a litter only once every two years. A typical rattler lives only about twelve years, and a six-foot-long snake would be very old and a very rare sight.

Our own snake surprised me, as its body was limestone gray with dark markings. It was perfectly docile, but attentive, as I took pictures. This was my first sighting of a live rattlesnake, and I've lived for twenty years in the Mississippi River blufflands.

The **National Historic Trail of Tears** follows Route 146 from Golconda on the Ohio River to Cape Girardeau in Missouri. Trails follow the ground route taken in the winter of 1838 and 1839 during the forced removal of the Cherokee Nation from Tennessee to Oklahoma. For more on the Cherokee Trail of Tears, be sure to visit the excellent interpretive display at the visitor center at Trail of Tears State Park just north of Cape Girardeau, Missouri.

Union State Tree Nursery is located just inside Trail of Tears State Forest. Seedlings, including bald cypress and northern species of oak, are raised here for the state forests and the public.

――――――――――――― ✹ ―――――――――――――

Exit east of Trail of Tears State Forest and go to Hwy. 127.
Turn north to visit the villages and sights
of Alto Pass and Pomona.

Alto Pass, Illinois
Population 500

Collectors visiting Alto Pass will enjoy Austin's Antiques, one of the largest antique shops in southern Illinois. Several more antique shops occupy turn-of-the-century buildings. Residents today are mostly retired or employed in Carbondale and other nearby cities. The knob where Alto ("high") Pass is located and Bald Knob, the site of Bald Knob Cross, are the highest points in southern Illinois.

Three wineries featuring award-winning wines are clustered in the Alto Pass/Pomona/Cobden area. Most of the local fruit is harvested by migrant workers.

"This is a midwest niche market," Mark Renzaglia tells me as we sit near his vines at Alto Pass. "We're not trying to compete with the California wines. It's hard to compete with traditions already firmly established—the traditions of places like France, California, Italy or Australia. Also we are not able to grow *vitas viniferous* grapes which are traditionally what the most famous wines are made from. But we compete very well with the Missouri and Indiana wineries."

WHAT TO SEE IN ALTO PASS

Bald Knob Cross 🄰

618-893-2344. 112-foot-tall porcelain-faced cross, the tallest Christian edifice in North America. Visible across the rolling tops of the Shawnee Hills.

My favorite view of Bald Knob Cross is southeast of the Alto Pass on Skyline Drive. A small park there offers an overlook which is fascinating not only for the spectacle of a huge man-made structure visible in the distance, but for the unobstructed view of the sharp, tree-covered, alternating hills and valleys of the wild Shawnee National Forest and Trail of Tears State Forest.

I arrived just before sunset painted the sky and shared the view with Joe Bennett and his wife. We stood on the edge of a limestone precipice and Joe described how native Indians harvested entire herds of buffalo by forcing them over the cliff to their death on the bare rock below. Joe, retired from a career with the electrical company, is responsible for lighting Bald Knob Cross.

"My story goes back to when I was a teenager," he began, in a voice that was surprisingly deep and soft. "At that time I sang in a gospel quartet. A gentleman by the name of Wayman Presley contacted me about promoting

According to local historians, Native Americans drove buffalo herds over this high, sharp escarpment near Alto Pass in the Shawnee Hills. A rocky plateau below assured an instant death for the terrified animals.

his project to build the largest cross in North America. He came to our appearances and spoke to our audiences about his dream of building the cross. From those talks, he was able to find 115 people willing to donate $100 each to the project for buying the land. The cross was completed in 1952. Later I started serving on the Board of Directors. That's how far back I go with the Cross!

"Many nationally prominent people have spoken to anywhere from 5,000 to 15,000 people during Easter sunrise services at the foot of the cross."

SPECIAL EVENTS IN ALTO PASS

Easter: *Easter Sunrise Service at Bald Knob Mountain.* Free admission. Celebrity guest pastors. 618-893-2344.

Pomona, Illinois

WHAT TO SEE IN POMONA

Pomona Natural Bridge Recreational Area ⓯

618-687-1731. A mini-park (.5 acre) set in a beech/hickory forest. A short (.3-mile) scenic foot trail leads to the 90-foot natural rock bridge that arches 25 feet above a small stream. Be observant, as at several points along the trail, the slope exceeds 20%. Picnicking.

**Return south on Route 127 through Jonesboro and Anna.
Jonesboro is at the junction of Hwys. 127 and 146;
Anna is east of Jonesboro on 146.**

Jonesboro, Illinois
Population 1700

Jonesboro has the only English "roundabout" I've ever seen in the Midwest! Let the roundabout lead you around to the north exit to visit the **Historic Fairgrounds**, where

115

Jonesboro hosted one of the 1856 Lincoln-Douglas debates. For visitor information, call 618-833-6311.

An historic marker at the park notes that the debates were held on the afternoon of September 15, 1858. Abe Lincoln and Stephen A. Douglas met in the third of seven senatorial debates. Lincoln lost the senatorial election but gained such prominence nationally that he was elected to the presidency two years later. The marker continues, "Lincoln was truly Illinois' gift, a man for the ages."

As an interesting aside, during the Civil War, Jonesboro was the only town in the North to be occupied by Union troops in order to enforce loyalty. This is a reminder that nowhere else in the nation was there as much diversity of opinion regarding slavery. Whereas in most areas state lines drew fairly sharp borders between pro- and anti-slavery forces, in southern Illinois the overlap was nearly 100 miles. Within this broad buffer, opinions differed strongly from neighbor to neighbor and town to town.

SPECIAL EVENTS IN JONESBORO

Late November to late December: *Holiday Wreaths & Pines.* 1¼ miles west of Jonesboro on Highway 146. Late 1800s farm featuring horse-drawn covered wagon rides, and pick and cut your own Christmas tree. Hot apple cider. Monday-Saturday 9 a.m. to dark. Sundays, noon to dark. 618-833-2845.

Anna, Illinois
Population 4900

Anna adjoins Jonesboro and boasts many Victorian houses.

SPECIAL EVENTS IN ANNA

November 11: *Veterans Day Parade.* Parade begins at 2 p.m. from the city park entrance on Davie St. and follows Main St. to the high school.

○

Continue on Hwy. 146 to I-57 and go south toward Ullin.

Ullin, Illinois

Ullin was one of the many railroad towns that sprang up as the Illinois Central connected this area to Chicago. Today many residents of small towns in the Cache River area work at Cape Girardeau, Carbondale, and Murphysboro.

The Best Western Cheekwood Motel in Ullin makes a good headquarters for anyone interested in exploring the Cache River Wetlands, the city of Cairo, Illinois, or the rest of southern Illinois. The Southernmost Illinois Tourism Bureau is also located at the motel. Pick up a brochure detailing recreational activities and trails in the **Cache River Wetlands**. Heron Pond, about 8 miles east of Ullin, is one of the main attractions of the **Cypress Creek National Wildlife Refuge**.

A BRIEF HISTORY OF THE CACHE RIVER WETLANDS

The first European settlers, arriving in this area in 1803, tried clearing small patches of the swampy bottomland along the Cache River for farming. The bottomland soils were rich, but too wet for farming, and settlers eventually turned their efforts to harvesting timber. Sawmills popped up in the 1870s and large quantities of timber were harvested for lumber, veneer for manufacturing baskets and boxes, railroad ties, mine timbers and charcoal. Large-scale drainage and land clearing efforts to develop farmland began in the 1900s.

The Main Brothers Lumber Company, headquartered in Karnak, made packaging crates until after World War II, selling many to the Sears and Roebuck Company. As cypress trees tolerate water very well and are weather- and termite-resistant, many barns and foundations were made of cypress.

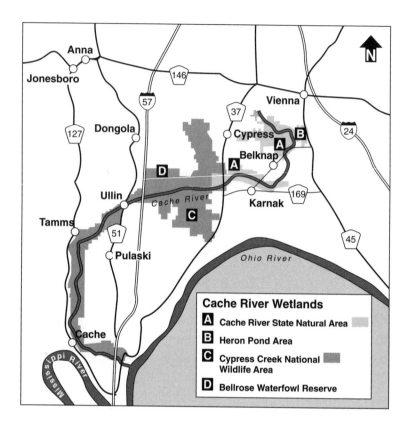

Today, preservation and restoration of the Cache River Wetlands is a joint project of state, federal and private agencies.

Cache River State Natural Area (A)

A 9,402-acre natural area located in Johnson and Pulaski counties. Twenty-three state threatened or endangered plant and animal species and several state champion trees are located in this wildlife refuge. Birding, hunting, wildlife-watching, and hiking on 9 miles of designated foot trails. Site Superintendent, Cache River State Natural Area, Rt. 2, Box 2, Belknap, Illinois 62908, 618-634-9678.

This is designated as a National Natural Landmark because it contains true southern swamps at the northern portion of their range and striking examples of the high quality wetland communities that once covered the area. Bald cypress and tupelo gum swamps in the area contain trees more than 1,000 years old.

Heron Pond Area, Cache River State Natural Area (B) 🜟

Access: Follow signs off Karnak-Belknap Road north to parking area.

This is the most impressive and popular of three nature preserves for visitors, with a floating half-mile boardwalk that takes visitors to an observation deck in the center of the swamp. Look for several species of heron and egret, pileated woodpeckers and vultures along with the occasional migrating osprey or overwintering bald eagle. At about the third curve in the boardwalk is a bush right next to the railing. According to the site superintendent, this bush shelters the single most photographed prothonotary warbler nest in America, having graced even the pages of *National Geographic*.

As you cross the Cache River bridge on the way to the boardwalk, note the huge cypress tree roots visible on the banks. The deep, stabilizing taproot of the cypress accounts for its success in damp areas. Less firmly rooted trees will tip and expose their roots as soil erodes away. Note, too, that many of the cypress trees look half dead—as tall as they are, they are often struck by lightning. A portion of the tree dies, but the rest lives.

The largest trees in this area are about 500 years old. You'll notice that large areas of the swamp will often contain similar sized trees. This is because cypress trees require dry periods in order for new seedlings to sprout. In some years there were no dry periods, so "recruitment" of young cypress was not possible. There have essentially been no new recruitments since the locks and dams were built in the 1930s and '40s to permanently control water levels in the area.

Another tree found commonly on the drier slopes and plateaus of southern Illinois is the sycamore, with its star-shaped leaf. It's easy to identify by white areas high on the trunk where it has shed its bark. Sycamore is often used to make student desks because the wood is so hard it's difficult to carve in.

Cypress Creek National Wildlife Area (C)

U.S. Fish and Wildlife Refuge. Rt. 1, Box 53D, Ullin, IL 62992, 618-634-2231.

Part of the Cache River Wetlands Project. Cypress Creek is a tributary of the Cache River within the refuge. Canoe rental and shuttle information are available in the wildlife area or at the Cheekwood Best Western Hotel.

Most old-growth trees in the area are accessible only by canoe. Water in the swamp is usually 2-6 feet deep. Cypress Creek National Wildlife area has been designated as a RAMSAR Site, an international designation for wetlands of significant importance, especially for waterfowl. There are only fourteen such sites in the United States.

Bellrose Waterfowl Reserve (D) *(Call the refuge for access.)* A gravel path through the preserve is big enough for a car, but it is probably better just to carry along binoculars and walk the one-mile track. The first field, of clover, provides shelter for the ground-roosting northern harrier or marsh hawk. Fields that look like cranberry bogs are filled with water and drained periodically to provide habitat for ducks and geese during appropriate seasons. An active eagle's nest is visible from the gravel roadway. In 1996 it was the first documented active nest in the Cache River Wetlands since 1909.

Smartweed, duckweed, and wild millet are planted in the refuge for waterfowl and shorebirds. (Per acre, wild millet produces more grain than a field of cultivated corn!) The bogs are drained in the spring so the shorebirds can eat the invertebrates (insects) left behind for needed protein. Food is important because of heavy physiological demands on birds during migration. In addition, females are preparing to lay eggs and males are undergoing a molt.

Expect to see a huge diversity of shorebirds in the spring as many species come up the Mississippi and stage here. During February and March, look for snow geese and up to 25,000 to 30,000 Canada geese in fields with open water. Wintering geese maintain waterproofing by mixing fresh water with preening oils, so it is not cold weather that sends them south for the winter but the search for fresh water.

— ⚙ —

Rejoin the Great River Road (Illinois Route 3) at Cairo.

Alexander County, Illinois

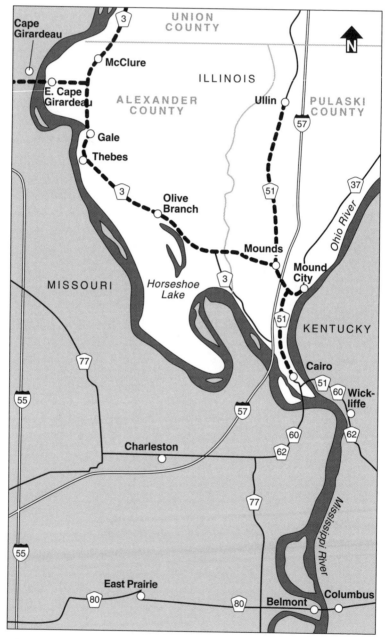

8

Alexander & Pulaski Counties, Illinois

This southernmost portion of Illinois sits approximately 50 miles farther south than Richmond, Virginia, its soils nourished since prehistoric times by flood waters of the ancient Mississippi, Ohio, and Tennessee Rivers. Agriculture is the main industry, with soybeans, corn, wheat, and cotton sown and harvested in rapid succession during all four seasons of the year. Fields smolder in the fall as many farmers resort to "slash and burn" techniques better known in South American rainforests. Time is money and there is no time to spare for traditional plowing and disking.

The brief, high drive between Gale and Thebes provides rare, sparkling views of the river, especially at sunset. The main channel is just offshore, and you will see tows that average seven barges long and four across—a reminder that you are now on the Lower River, where tows can be as large as the captain believes he can handle—typically around 30 barges, but possibly twice that many.

HISTORICAL NOTES ON ALEXANDER COUNTY

In the early 19th century, southern Illinois was known as Little Egypt because of its agricultural productivity. After the Big Snow of 1830 killed most of the seed corn in the north, farmers were forced to purchase grain from southern counties—like Jacob's brothers visiting Egypt. This explains the Egyptian names of some southern river towns: Cairo, Thebes, and Memphis.

At the start of the Civil War, it was obvious to both North and South that Cairo would be pivotal to controlling the Mississippi River. As shots rang out at Fort Sumter, Federal and Confederate troops raced for this strategic location at the confluence of the Ohio and the Mississippi. The Federal troops arrived just 11 hours before the Confederates, time enough to secure the town as northern territory. The Confederates were halted just to the south, at Columbus, Kentucky, and established their first fort on the lower river there. From 1860 to the present, Cairo has been county seat for Alexander County, assuming the duties once conducted in the little courthouse that still sits on the river bluff at Thebes.

Thebes, Illinois

While Thebes does not offer any amenities for the traveler, it is an historic river town with convenient river access. The state of Illinois recently built a small park on the north end of town, just off Highway 3, with picnic tables and a wooden walkway toward the river. Thebes' main street dips steeply down the bluffside to the riverfront and an undeveloped riverside park. Through the years, much of the lower area where the town was originally located has eroded into the river.

HISTORICAL NOTES ON THEBES

Thebes was the government seat for Alexander County from 1845 to 1865. The 1845 Greek Revival-style Courthouse perches at the top edge of the bluff; a sign posted nearby reads: *This courthouse, completed in 1848, was the county seat of Alexander County until 1860, when the county seat was moved to Cairo. It was constructed of local sandstone, hewn timbers, hand-sawed boards and with a split shingle roof. Dred Scott was imprisoned in the dungeon below. He was a fugitive slave for whom the Judge's decision was made establishing a Negro's right to his own person.*

The Dred Scott Case, involving the status of slavery in the federal territories, was argued before the U.S. Supreme Court in 1856-57. After Scott, a slave from Missouri, was taken by his master to the Illinois and Wisconsin territory, he sued for freedom based on his residence in a free state and territory.

The Supreme Court's southern majority declared that the Missouri Compromise, which prohibited slavery in new territories, was unconstitutional and that Congress had no power to limit slavery in the territories. Congress, it held, was powerless to restrict property—in this case, slaves. This decision further inflamed the sectional controversy leading to the Civil War.

The Thebes Courthouse sits high on a bluff above the river in Thebes.

— ⚙ —

Follow Hwy. 3 south from Thebes to Olive Branch, about 10 miles. Thebes is 30 miles south of Tower Rock and 23 miles north of Cairo.

Olive Branch, Illinois

For accommodations, hunting guides and other information, contact the Olive Branch Chamber of Commerce, Olive Branch, IL 62969, 618-776-5541.

Olive Branch is a small village with several large cafés located north of Cairo and just outside Horseshoe Lake Conservation area.

WHAT TO SEE IN THE OLIVE BRANCH AREA

Horseshoe Lake Conservation Area　　△ ⹁ ⸶ ⯭

Located northwest of Cairo, southwest of Olive Branch on Highway 3, 618-776-5541. Two camping areas, both with electricity. 80 sites. Dump station. Office hours, 10:30-3:30. 50% discount for seniors. No hiking trails, but an auto trail around the lake.

Horseshoe Lake's large wetland stands of tupelo, swamp cottonwood and cypress trees are home to bald eagles and nearly 150,000 Canada geese that winter here. The camping area is well-maintained, with RV sites and fishing docks located right along the cypress-choked 2,400-acre lake. The average depth of the lake is 5 feet and it offers excellent crappie fishing. During our visit, a family had just found a huge black snake sunning on the doorstep of their RV—a harmless water snake, Superintendent Russ Garrison assured them. In 28 years, he's never seen a cottonmouth.

We heard geese honking and saw cormorants as Russ related the history of Horseshoe Lake. The Conservation area was originally purchased in 1929 with the objective of conserving goose habitat. The effort produced the opposite of what they planned: In the 1930s and '40s this was the ONLY possible shelter for the geese along the river, and they were so concentrated and so easily hunted that by the 1940s only about 18,000 geese were left in the refuge.

For a period of time after the '40s, hunting was banned to allow geese a chance to repopulate the area. Today, several more wetland preserves have been established in Southern Illinois. Geese winter at Rend Lake, Crab Orchard, Union County Refuge and Horseshoe, then fly north to summer on Hudson Bay and James Bay in Canada. Although water will freeze in southern Illinois, swimming geese keep large areas free of ice as they require fresh water for preening, drink-

INSIGHT

Cypress Trees at Horseshoe Lake

Four sawmills once operated around Horeseshoe Lake. Today's old growth trees (some as old as 800 years) were left by loggers only because they were considered undesirable for logging. Park Superintendent Russ Garrison noted that until about 1940, the trees were growing very well, but since the 1940s, when the water level started being artificially maintained at a steady level, "you almost need a magnifying glass to count the tree rings." Before the 1940s the lake alternated naturally between wet and dry phases. Water loving cypress trees require dry land for sprouting, so more trees grew around the edges of the lake, where the land dried periodically, than in the middle.

Look for cypress with bark gnawed away by beavers. A tree that has been completely *girdled* (the bark chewed off all the way around) will die. The park has started a program to trap and remove beaver, as remaining cypress are too precious to be lost. As explained above, cypress regeneration requires alternating periods of high and low water, so damaged trees in the lake can never be replaced under current management practices.

Ancient cypress trees

ing, feeding, and waterproofing. The park maintains about 1000 acres of winter wheat to provide feed for them.

Hunting is now allowed in season and many hunting camps and cabins circle the refuge. Perhaps 60 American bald eagles winter in the park, and have for about six years, harvesting geese crippled during the hunting season.

To visit the Mound City National Cemetery, follow signs on an unnamed blacktop road from Horseshoe Lake to Mounds and then to Mound City on Hwys. 51 and 37.

Mound City, Illinois

While Mound City was not in the combat theater during the Civil War, it was an important staging point. Hospitals were established at both Mound City and six miles south at Cairo. The Mound City hospital, staffed by Roman Catholic nurses, was one of the largest in the west, accommodating 1000 to 1500 patients. It was natural to locate a cemetery nearby.

Mound City National Cemetery

Four miles east of I-57 from exit #8. At the junction of Highways 51 and 37.

The National Cemetery contains markers for 6,000 Union and Confederate soldiers.

Continue to Cairo on Hwy. 51.

Cairo, Illinois
Population 4600

Southernmost Illinois Tourism Bureau, P.O. Box 278, Exit 18 off I-57, Ullin, IL, 800-248-4373. A good central place to stay while exploring southernmost Illinois is the Best Western Cheekwood Inn in Ullin, 800-528-1234.

In 1924, Edna Ferber researched her novel *Showboat* in the city of Cairo (prounounced *CARE-o*). The little girl in the book, Kim, is named for **K**entucky, **I**llinois, and **M**issouri. Today, the waters that surround Cairo still roil with

The Ironclads of Mound City, Illinois

The "ironclad" steamboats which made victory possible for the north were designed by James Buchanan Eads, the same engineer who built Eads Bridge in St. Louis. The *Mound City*, the *Cairo*, and the *Cincinnati* were all built at the shipyards in Mound City in 1862. The rest of the fleet was built near St. Louis. Andrew H. Foote was the commander of the ironclad fleet.

A scale model of the *Cairo*, the first ironclad boat sunk by a mine device, is displayed at the Custom House in Cairo, Illinois. Commissioned in January, the *Cairo* sank the following December. Armored to the waterline but vulnerable underneath, it lay in the mud of the Yazoo River for 100 years after the battle at Vicksburg, Mississippi, before it was retrieved and restored. It is now displayed with many artifacts in the Federal Military Park at Vicksburg.

There is a walk-in model of an ironclad boat at the Mud Island Museum in Memphis. Modifications to the ordinary steamboat included such design changes as adding 2½ inches of iron over 2 feet of solid oak and boxing in paddlewheels. An ironclad built especially for the war was designed with its paddlewheel in the center of the boat for added protection.

Pilot houses were completely boarded in except for eye-slots. On new warboats, the pilot house was reduced to narrow windows elevated just off the deck. It was the ironclads that allowed General Grant's men to run the gauntlet past Island 10 (near Tiptonville, Tennessee), opening the Mississippi River to northern troops.

Painting of iron-clad boats with Cairo at the skyline.

tows and barges heading up the Ohio and the Mississippi. No river trip is complete without a visit to see for oneself the blue waters of the Ohio pushing southward alongside the muddy waters of the Mississippi at Fort Defiance, a small park at the very tip of Cairo. The Ohio River flows into the Mississippi river from the east side of Cairo; the Mississippi flows along its west bank.

Though Cairo is no longer the bustling city it was immediately after the Civil War, it is still worth a visit as a nod to its place in Civil War history. Many attractions are truly beautiful and interesting relics of the city's changing fortunes. A small cadre of history buffs are restoring, almost singlehandedly, the historic Custom House.

HISTORICAL NOTES ON CAIRO

From the historical marker at the entrance to Fort Defiance: *Pierre Francois Xavier, a Jesuit priest, reported as early as 1721 that the confluence of the Ohio and Mississippi Rivers would be a strategic location for a settlement and fortification. Later, in 1818, the Illinois Territorial Legislature incorporated the city and Bank of Cairo. But the city did not begin to prosper until completion of the Illinois Central Railroad from Chicago to Cairo in 1854.*

When the Civil War began, both northern and southern strategists realized the importance of Cairo. In 1861, just days after the bombardment of Fort Sumter, Federal troops arrived to hold Cairo for the Union. The soldiers set up camp at the south end of the city and Cairo flourished as a troop supply center for General Ulysses S. Grant.

Ulysses Simpson Grant (1822-1885), a graduate of West Point, directed his first battle as a new Brigadier General at Belmont, Missouri, just south of Cairo, on November 9, 1861. On April 9, 1865, he accepted the surrender of Robert E. Lee's Confederate Army at Appomatox. His two-volume *Memoirs* of his battles in the Civil War were skillfully written and rank among the great military narratives of history.

Grant was rewarded for his role in the Federal victory by being awarded the rank of full General—the first civilian since George Washington to receive that rank. Grant was the 18th president of the United States from 1869 to 1877.

There are few signs in downtown Cairo directing the traveler to historic Civil War sites, which include the locations of U. S. Grant's hotel, the headquarters for the Western Army, and the field where troops camped during the western campaign.

Ulysses S. Grant

Cairo's southern levee is still located at what was the southern edge of the peninsula at the time Grant's troops were headquartered in Cairo. The barracks for the Federal troops were located in the field south of Second Street, where a few warehouses sit today.

Grant lived at the St. Charles Hotel on Second Street. As you walk along Second Street, the foundation stones for the St. Charles are still visible (at B on the map), though unmarked. The hotel would have overlooked a sea of white troop tents.

Continue following Second Street to the Ohio River Levee (Ohio Street). Even today, the cruising steamboats dock at the area near the corner of 6th and Ohio Streets where all 50 state flags flutter on the levee wall. Right across the street from these flags is approximately where Grant's headquarters were located on the second floor of the City Bank of Cairo—a city garage is on the site now, as the historic buildings along Ohio Street were razed in the early 1960s.

Grant's desk is on display at the Custom House Museum. It and some eating utensils carved from horn were the only Grant artifacts I found still preserved and on public display in Cairo.

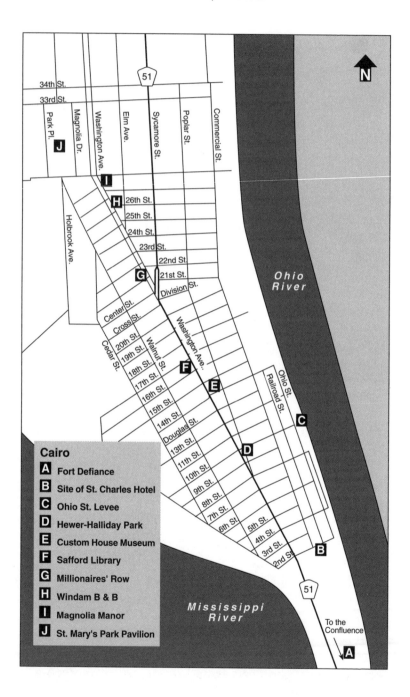

Cairo

- **A** Fort Defiance
- **B** Site of St. Charles Hotel
- **C** Ohio St. Levee
- **D** Hewer-Halliday Park
- **E** Custom House Museum
- **F** Safford Library
- **G** Millionaires' Row
- **H** Windam B & B
- **I** Magnolia Manor
- **J** St. Mary's Park Pavilion

WHAT TO SEE IN THE CAIRO AREA

Fort Defiance (A)

A large riverside park located on U.S. Highway 51 1.3 miles south of Cairo. Public boat ramp, picnicking. 618-734-3015.

Cairo was referred to as Fort Defiance during its occupation by the Union Army during the Civil War. To visit the park and witness the confluence of the Ohio and Mississippi Rivers, drive south through Cairo and stay in the right lane on Highway 51 until after the first bridge (to Kentucky). A second bridge goes to Missouri, but continue to the park, which is clearly signed. No fort was ever located in this large open public park and, in fact, as recently as the Civil War, this sandy gift of two great rivers did not even exist. The park is regularly inundated by high water.

Normally the Ohio waters, from the east, ripple blue alongside the brown Mississippi, but during my visit a steady wind had so stirred up the water that the famous blue/brown of the two-great rivers was not visible—the Ohio was actually much browner than the Mississippi.

As you stand at this confluence, be conscious of the fact that 60% of the water that flows through the United States must come past this point. Because the Tennessee and Cumberland Rivers flow north into the Ohio River, even much of the deep south drains out here. The Mississippi seldom freezes south of the confluence.

Fort Defiance, overlooking the confluence of the Ohio River (on the left) and the Mississippi River (on the right).

133

INSIGHT

Tributaries of the Mississippi River

The longest stream of water in the United States is the **Missouri River**, which begins at Three Forks, Montana (elevation 4,032 feet) and flows 2,714 miles to near St. Louis, Missouri. Many people consider the Missouri to be the main reach of the Mississippi River! The combined reach of the Missouri and the Mississippi (from St. Louis to the Gulf) is 3,741 miles—a length exceeded only by the Amazon and Nile rivers.

The **Mississippi**, from its source at Lake Itasca in Minnesota to the Gulf of Mexico, is 2,348 miles long, several hundred miles shorter than in days of Mark Twain. Even today it varies plus-or-minus 30 to 50 miles each year.

The **Ohio River** is the Mississippi's second major tributary. It is formed in Pittsburgh, Pennsylvania, by the junction of the Allegheny and Monongahela River and travels about 980 miles to Cairo and the Mississippi River. Today's Ohio River Basin is approximately at the northern extremity of the ancient shallow sea that is represented today by the Gulf of Mexico!

The **Arkansas River** begins in the Rocky Mountains in Colorado and meanders 1,450 miles through Kansas, Oklahoma, and Arkansas to empty into the Mississippi.

In all, some 250 Mississippi tributaries drain a total of more than 1,247,000 square miles—more than half of the nation's landmass!

During the Mississippi River flood of 1993, it wasn't just the Mississippi flooding that wreaked havoc, it was the flooding of all the tributaries! At one point, the volume of water flowing past St. Louis was eleven times the volume of Niagara Falls!!

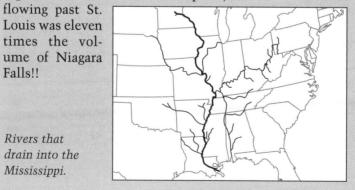

Rivers that drain into the Mississippi.

The Ohio Street Levee (C)

Levees completely encircle the city, and during great floods all highways are blocked, isolating Cairo temporarily as an island. Several former residents recalled that in flood times, one has to look *up* to see boats over the tops of the levee walls. At such times, the Mississippi backs up into the Ohio.

Hewer-Halliday Park (D)

Washington Avenue and Poplar Street.

This tiny park, which is surrounded by churches, is home to a sculpture by George Grey Bernard that was displayed at the World's Fair in St. Louis. Considered to be one of the finest nudes in the country, the sculpture has been moved several times because, as my guide related, the church ladies "did not appreciate having to see the man's bare behind every day."

Custom House Museum (E)

1400 Washington Avenue, 618-734-1840.

This museum recalls Cairo's heyday just before the Civil War, when the city was made a Port of Delivery, part of the collection district of New Orleans. A Surveyor of Customs was appointed to inspect and collect fees on goods at this point of entry. The Custom House was begun in 1867 and completed in 1872 by A. B. Mullett, architect for the U.S. Treasury Department. Mullett also designed the San Francisco Mint. The first floor was originally a post office, so its modern restoration includes a representative post office. Government offices were located on the second floor and a U.S. District Courtroom on the third floor.

Notice the unique "barrel vaulting" in the ceiling bricks visible through an opening. The barrel-sized arches provided extra strength to support the upper stories of the building. An 1890 telephone booth in the lobby includes lace curtains and a storm window. There are many artifacts and photos from Cairo's history, including a scale model of the ironclad gunboat, the *Cairo*.

A. B. Safford Memorial Public Library (F)　　　⚑

1609 Washington Avenue.

The Safford Public Library is as much a museum as a library. Sculptor Janet Scudder created the statue, *Fighting Boys*, in front of the Queen Anne-style building. An almost identical statue is at the Chicago Art Museum—but minus the fig leaves and garlands.

In the room on the right of the entryway are pictures of the old County Courthouses: Unity 1833 to 1845, Thebes 1845 to 1860, and Cairo 1860 to the present. The round, glass-covered table is a gambling table from a steamboat.

The Tiffany clock on the stairway to the second floor of the library is one of only four in the world. Its cut-glass pendulum is filled with mercury. The mercury rises and falls with changes in air pressure, and the clock keeps perfect time.

Notice that the wooden ceiling in the auditorium, on the left at the top of the stairs, has no grain—it is tupelo gum wood. The big chandelier came from the old Cairo Opera House. On the right side of the hallway is the climate-controlled Special Collections Room with over 600 Civil War and genealogy books for research, including an 1885 to 1895 diary written by Cairo resident Maud Rittenhouse, which was edited by Richard L. Strout and became the bestselling book, *Maud*.

A memorial outside to local resident Mary Jane Stafford commemorates the first woman in the west to organize camp and hospital relief under General Grant's personal command. Eventually she became one of the first woman physicians of her day.

Millionaire's Row (G)

Washington Avenue stretches north of the library to become known as Millionaire's Row—a very beautiful boulevard with many Victorian mansions and huge trees.

Windam Bed & Breakfast (H)   ↑▪

2606 Washington Avenue.

This privately owned Victorian brick B&B was built about 1876 by Thomas Halliday, a mayor of Cairo and Illinois Senator who lived here with his wife and 10 children. It is listed on the National Register of Historic Places and has been restored to almost museum quality. Pictures in the entryway date from 1600 to 1880.

Magnolia Manor (I)   ↑▪

2700 Washington Avenue. Listed on the National Register of Historic Places. Small entry fee.

This is an Italianate mansion built in 1869 by a miller who prospered by providing much of the hardtack for the northern army. A magnolia tree, with its fleshy leaves, stands out front, and much of the furniture inside is from the original home. Note that the chairs at the dining room table were fitted and built to match the size of each person—some taller, some shorter or wider. Also note the hand carving on all the furniture.

St. Mary's Park Pavilion (J)

A 13-acre park between Magnolia Dr. and Park Place West, near 33rd and Highland, one block off Washington Avenue.

The large pavilion is called the Roosevelt Pavilion in honor of a visit from Theodore Roosevelt in 1907. In addition to Roosevelt, Presidents William Taft, Andrew Jackson, Jefferson Davis and Bill Clinton have visited Cairo.

---------------- ✿ ----------------

Leave Cairo on Hwy. 3 north of town and drive north to Hwy. 146. Cross the river at East Cape Girardeau, IL, for a visit to Cape Girardeau, Missouri and Trail of Tears State Park.

Cape Girardeau and
Perry Counties, Missouri

9

Cape Girardeau and Perry Counties, Missouri

Cape Girardeau, Missouri
Population 34,436

Cape Girardeau seems a bustling community after visiting Cairo, Illinois, and the small towns tucked away in the Shawnee Forest. Nearby Trail of Tears State Park is the only Missouri State Park located along the Mississippi River.

The city boasts two major hospitals and a new 13.5 million dollar convention complex located near the 8,000-student Southeast Missouri University. When orienting oneself to Cape's busy streets, it helps to remember that three main roads (Independence, William, and Broadway) start in downtown Cape Girardeau at the river and lead west out of town toward Interstate 55.

A BRIEF HISTORY OF CAPE GIRARDEAU
In 1792, the Spanish transfered military power in the area to Don Louis Lorimier, a French fur trader and military governor. In the mid-1700s, it was a young French ensign stationed at Kaskaskia, Illinois, who lent his name to the city. Jean Baptiste Girardot, from the French Royale Troupe de Marine, crossed the river to establish a trading post in the shelter of the large "cape" or promontory of rock that projected out into the river.

Early in the nineteenth century, Shawnee/Delaware and Sac/Mesquakie (Fox) Indians were resettled by the American government to Missouri, helping to form a buffer between settlers and the native Missouri Indians.

During the 1820s, Sioux rights to land in Missouri were sold for $400 in gifts, the Sac received $7,500 for a portion of their lands, and other tribes received a total of $4,520. Just north of Cape Girardeau, at Moccasin Springs and opposite today's Trail of Tears State Park, the suffering Cherokee nation crossed the river during a forced march from Georgia and eastern Tennessee to Oklahoma. By 1836, all Indian tribes were removed from the state to lands farther west.

WHAT TO SEE IN CAPE GIRARDEAU

Capaha City Park and Rose Garden (A)

Since the 1930s, Cape Girardeau has been known as the City of Roses, thanks in part to a 10-mile-long rose garden which stretched from Cape to Jackson until 1968. Red roses bloomed on one side of the road, white on the other, as a memorial to those who had died on both sides during the Civil War. Today, hundreds of rose bushes are still planted annually in the city, and more than 80 varieties bloom in the Rose Garden in Capaha Park.

Capaha Park is one of 23 parks in the city, and is named for the Capaha Indians who camped here. "Capaha" translates into "downstream." As many as 20 different tribes have lived in the vicinity.

Cape River Heritage Museum (B)

At the old Cape Fire Station, just off Broadway, 573-334-0405. Open seasonally from 11 a.m. to 4 p.m. Wednesday through Saturday, 1 to 4 p.m. Sunday. River-related and historical artifacts are displayed.

The Common Pleas Courthouse and Park (C)

At Themis Street, between Spanish and Lorimier Streets.

The Courthouse was built in 1854 at an Indian council site overlooking the river. At one time, runaway slaves held

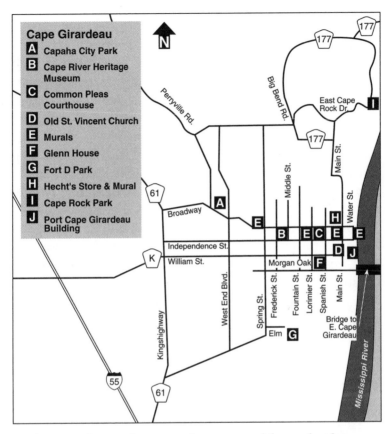

in the courthouse dungeon dug a tunnel from the dungeon to the river and escaped. Joseph Lansmon, the stonemason responsible for the courthouse, also built Old St. Vincent's Church and the Seminary at the foot of the bridge.

Old St. Vincent Church (D)

Corner of William and Main Streets.

Built in 1853 of Renaissance-Gothic design, Old St. Vincent Church is on the National Register of Historic Places. More than 100 medieval designs and plaster masks decorate both the interior and exterior of the building. A nearby marker notes that Spanish Street is part of *El Camino Real*— or King's Highway—which was constructed in the 1790s by the Spanish to provide a roadway from New Orleans to St. Louis.

Murals (E)

At the flood wall on Water Street, just opposite the Main Street Jewish Synagogue, is a chart noting historic high water marks. Also painted on the wall is one of eight murals that decorate Cape Girardeau. This mural commemorates famous Missourians, and the list is a long one! T.S. Eliot, George Washington Carver, Scott Joplin, Burt Bacharach, Dale Carnegie, Walter Cronkite, Harry Truman, Mark Twain, Tennessee Williams, Eugene Field and many more! Rush Limbaugh is from Cape Girardeau and astronaut Linda Goodwin is from nearby Oak Ridge.

Another mural is located on the University campus, and there is a mural on the river side of the floodwall. See the map for other mural sites. The floodwall in Cape Girardeau is 21 feet high, with a footing that is 21 feet deep and at a slant toward the river for extra strength. It is 1.5 miles long and cost more than $4 million dollars to build. It withstood the flood of 1993.

Glenn House (F)

573-334-1177. National Historic Register Home. Open 1 to 4 p.m. Thursday through Sunday, May to December.

This is a restored Victorian Home built by Edwin Branch Dean, an architect who designed many of Cape's outstanding nineteenth-century dwellings. Notice architecture that made the home comfortable in this hot climate: high ceilings collected the heat overhead while little windows over the doors allowed it to escape. Every room has a door to the exterior. The central hallway is reminiscent of the "dog trot" design of a two-room log cabin; the central hallway served to catch the river breeze and draw air through the house.

Fort D Park (G)

Near May Green School at Giboney and Fort Streets (toward I-55) in the south end of town.

At the start of the Civil War, U.S. Grant was given command of troops encamped in Cape Girardeau. He ordered the establishment of four forts in Cape Girardeau in order to hold Cape Girardeau for the Union. In 1861, Grant's headquarters were established at today's 170-year old Port Cape Girardeau building. The town was called Camp Fremont at that time for Grant's commanding officer, Gen. John C. Fremont.

Hecht's Store & Mural (H)

The store was completed in 1928 by architect T. B. Barnett, who was inspired by the cathedrals in Rome and Paris. Be sure to check out the mosaic mural under the arched exterior foyer ceiling.

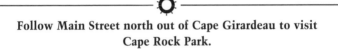

Follow Main Street north out of Cape Girardeau to visit Cape Rock Park.

Cape Rock Park (I)

There is only a small sign just north of town to indicate this park. A scenic overlook provides a panoramic view of the river and the rem-nants of Cape Rock, though little of the original cape remains; most of it was removed in the late 1800s for the Frisco railroad tracks. The rolling hills you'll see, with their rocky outcrops, are a portion of the Missouri Ozarks that continue into Illinois. If you visit in fall, expect the leaf colors to peak in mid-October.

WHERE TO STAY IN CAPE GIRARDEAU

There are several bed & breakfast inns in Cape Girardeau. I stayed at **Neumeyers B&B,** which introduced me to the low-slung Craftsman style of architecture. For information on accommodations, contact the Cape Girardeau Convention and Visitors Bureau, P.O. Box 617, 2121 Broadway, Cape Girardeau, MO 63702-0617, 800-777-0068 or 573-335-1631.

**Continue 10 miles north of Cape Girardeau
on Hwy. 177 to Trail of Tears State Park.**

Trail of Tears State Park

Equestrian trails (day use only). Picnicking, scenic overlooks, swimming, fishing, boating. Interpretive Center open April-September from 9 a.m. to 5 p.m. Monday through Saturday and noon to 5 p.m. on Sunday. In October the center is closed Monday and Tuesday. From November through March it is open from 10 a.m. to 4 p.m. Friday and Saturday, halfdays on Sundays and closed Monday through Thursday. Call for appointment, 573-334-1711.

The excellent Trail of Tears State Park Interpretive Center offers a multimedia interpretation of the **Cherokee Trail of Tears** and seasonal displays of plants and animals found in the park. In April, the park forests are abloom with redbud, dogwood, and flowering pears. Closer to the river, moist air nurtures a rare beech-tulip poplar forest. Away from the river, forests quickly change to the more common Ozark oak-hickory hardwood forest. An average tree height of 150 feet and a lack of oak stumps indicates that very little logging occurred in the area. The showy stand of Cucumber magnolia here is one of the finest in the state.

**Leave Trail of Tears State Park and travel north and west
on Hwy. 177. Turn right (north) on U.S. Hwy. 61
to Fruitland, then right (northeast) on Cty. C through
Pocahontas to Altenburg.**

Beyond the village of **Pocahontas**, population 125, the curvy road to Altenburg is exceptionally picturesque, dotted with one-lane bridges and red barns more typically seen in German communities of Wisconsin and Minnesota. Wisconsin is the only other place where I have seen distinctive red and white striped barns like those in Perry County.

Visits to Altenburg and Wittenberg are recommended for historical interest. The ghost town of Wittenberg, opposite Grand Tower, also has one of the best views of the landmark Tower Rock.

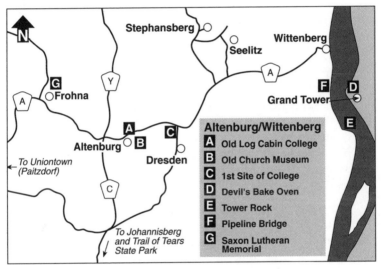

Altenburg, Missouri
Population 256

A sign outside Altenburg announces, "Saxony Lutheran Settlements. 150th Anniversary." Altenburg is named for the 1000-year-old city of Altenburg in the Saxony area near Leipzig in Germany. It is the saga of the early Saxons, who combined their fortunes to settle in this new and secluded paradise, that lends primary interest to the villages of Altenburg, on the top of the hill, and Wittenberg, six miles east at the river's edge. Here is the birthplace of the Lutheran Church – Missouri Synod.

The Cherokee Trail of Tears
Summarized from Missouri DNR sources

The pressure of white movement across Indian lands east of the Mississippi River was causing constant agitation by the early 1820s. When gold was discovered in Georgia on Cherokee land in 1828, the public clamor to remove the natives became irresistible for President Andrew Jackson.

General Winfield Scott's troops conducted the Cherokee roundup in Tennessee, Alabama, and North Carolina with military precision and forced 16,000 prisoners to march to stockades for confinement. The Indians offered little resistance and within two weeks the Cherokee were a captive nation.

Conditions in the stockades were primitive and unsanitary. A summer-long drought made drinking water scarce. Cholera and measles swept the stockade and 1600 died during the summer and autum of 1838.

A tape recording at the interpretive center records a story passed to a woman in 1932 from her mother:

When the soldiers came to our house, my father wanted to fight. My mother said if he did the soldiers would kill him. We surrendered without a fight. They drove us out of our house. My mother begged them to let her go back and get some bedding. They let her go back. She brought bedding and a few cooking utensils. She had to leave everything else behind. My father had a wagon pulled by two spans of oxen to pull us in. Eight of my brothers and sisters, a widow-woman and children rode with us. My father and mother walked all the way. The people got so tired of eating salt pork on the journey that my father would walk through the woods hunting for turkey and deer which he brought back to feed us. The camp was usually made somewhere where water was to be had. As we prepared to cook, other emigrants who had been forced from their homes without any cooking utensils came to use our pots and utensils. There was much sickness and many children died of whooping cough.

Nine thousand Cherokee began the journey west in October 1838. Four thousand more would start by the first week in December. Many were already weak and ill after months of confinement in stockades in Tennessee. Contingents of 1200 were marched across the Cumberland Range and across the Cumberland River near Nashville, Tennessee. As the first contingents crossed the Ohio River into Kentucky, the cold weather and difficult journey took an increasing toll on the weak and sick. Many died and were buried.

One by one the groups following the shorter land route moved through Southern Illinois through Golconda to Jonesboro and on to the river flats to await transportation across the Mississippi at two locations—one crossing was opposite today's Trail of Tears State Park and the other opposite Moccasin Springs near today's Cape Girardeau, 10 miles downriver. Some of the first to cross the river waited for as long as a month with little food or shelter for the entire contingent to join them on the Missouri shore.

Many emigrating Indians traveled across Missouri via Farmington, Caledonia, and St. James. Beyond these western settlements, their route followed Indian trails and postal roads. After reaching the corner of Arkansas they took various routes west into Indian Territory in present-day Oklahoma for a total distance of nearly 800 miles.

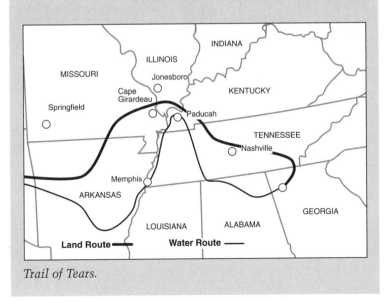

Trail of Tears.

WHAT TO SEE IN ALTENBURG

Old Log Cabin College (A)

A guided tour is available; check at the Old Church Museum.

Listed in the National Register of Historic Places, the College opened in 1839 as a Gymnasium, or Junior College, and offered six languages to its eleven students: Latin, Greek, Hebrew, German, French and English. Today at Southeast Missouri University in Cape Girardeau, they don't teach six different languages and there are 8,000 students!

Eventually the college was moved to St. Louis, where it became the Concordia Seminary. From this humble beginning, more than 10,000 pastors have been graduated from the Lutheran Church – Missouri Synod in the United States.

Old Church Museum (B)

The Museum is located across the street from the Old Log Cabin College, beside modern Trinity Lutheran church. It was constructed in 1845 of limestone hauled up to Altenburg by wheelbarrows and wagons and covered over with stucco. It is believed to be the oldest Protestant

Historian Vernon Myer, standing outside the Old Log Cabin College, is a direct descendant of the original Saxon settlers.

148

church still standing in Perry County. Many artifacts brought from Germany in 1839 are on display including old books and bibles, some from the 1700s. A time capsule removed from the old Wittenberg church shows evidence of having been flooded 16 times during its existence. Many of the earliest pastors are buried in the historic Trinity Lutheran cemetery nearby.

Leave Altenburg for Wittenberg, east on Cty. A.

Just at the Altenburg village limits, where the road dips into the valley, look off to the right to find two markers. The first is the original location of the spring that supplied water for the first settlers. The second marks the original location of the log seminary. Beyond the markers in the next valley you will see rooftops that are approximately where the Dresden congregation was located.

About three miles east of Trinity church is a small sign that reads "Stephansberg." Stop briefly to look at the valley off to the left. There, on a prominent knob, is where Martin Stephan's flock believed he planned to build his castle. Quarrying for the church and other stone buildings in Altenburg was done in this area. The rock was hauled by horse-drawn wagon up the hill three miles to Altenburg.

Just before arriving at Wittenberg, a signed gravel county road leads to a spot where you can view Tower Rock.

Tower Rock Viewing Area

The road to Tower Rock passes the anchor of the Pipeline Bridge, one of the longest bridges in the world at 600 feet. The pipeline, carrying natural gas from Texas, first lay on the bottom of the river, but it broke so often that this bridge was built to carry it. It's interesting to note

The Saxony Lutheran Story

In 1838 about 700 Germans left Saxony looking for a return to Luther's brand of Lutheranism under the fervent leadership of Rev. Martin Stephan. Four of their five ships landed in New Orleans. No word was ever received of the fifth ship and its 53 souls. The group continued by steamboat to St. Louis, where they arrived in January with a plan to buy land nearby — but with no immediate lodging or source of income to carry them through the remainder of the winter. Feeding and lodging the community depleted much of the communal funds.

With the arrival of spring, Stephan purchased 4,400 acres in east Perry County for about $9,000. Some 500 of the immigrants migrated downriver with him where the villages of Altenburg, Wittenberg, Paitzdorf, Dresden, Seelitz, Frohna, and Johannisberg (named after towns left behind in Germany) were planned by the five pastors who accompanied the group. Settlers were assigned communal plots of land under the authority of one of the pastors.

The first years were traumatic, with spiritual and physical despair that soon led to the ouster of Stephan and the near collapse of the entire community. An historical novel, *Except the Corn Die*, is available at the Old Church Museum in Altenburg. It brings to life the story of the settlement's early tragedies and eventual triumph.

that on the Missouri side, the bridge's anchor rests on bedrock 90 feet below the surface, but on the Illinois side, it's only about 30 feet to bedrock, indicating that the ancient river bed was once well west of, and much deeper than, the present river channel. [See picture on page 31.]

The main river channel, on the opposite side of Tower Rock, is one of the deeper spots on the river—about 100 feet deep. This rocky stretch of river, known as Thebes Gap, is the last area where southbound boats must maneuver over bedrock rather than silt.

The mangled debris of rock on the shore just downriver

from Tower Rock is the remnant of a bluff that once sat with a perfect cone of sand resting on top of it. "As if god had carefully poured the sand from a beaker," local historian Vernon Myer remembered. A dangerous whirlpool used to swirl in the small enclosed area between Tower Rock and the shore. It once swallowed up a wedding party unlucky enough to tip their boat as they tried to guide it toward shore. The bluff was quarried away, while Tower Rock was saved only by a government purchase after the Civil War because engineers thought it might make a good bridge support.

Although river flooding can cover the train tracks that run along the Missouri bluffs, in periods of very low water it is possible to walk across the rocks right to Tower Rock. DO NOT try to walk across unless the actual rock walkway has been laid bare, which only happens once or twice in a lifetime. The current is treacherous when water is flowing over the slippery rocks.

Wittenberg, Missouri

All of Wittenberg was under water during the floods of 1993 and '95, and now only a few houses still stand. One of those was originally a brewery, and its storage caverns are still visible in the bluffs. Two brewers had traveled together from Germany, one to settle here in Wittenberg, and the other, Anheuser, to try his luck in St. Louis. The Wittenberg brewer went broke and, needless to say, Anheuser prospered! In front of the brewery a square of large limestone blocks was once the village well.

A monument at the mouth of Brazeau Creek commemorates the landing of the Saxons. At one time, this was the site of a flour mill and a wharf area bustling with boats, workmen, and trade. A bank, stores, and homes all clattered with life along the edge of the bluff and flatland streets. I note in locals along the river a sadness at seeing river towns like Wittenberg wash away. With them goes a sense of place—personal histories and stories that no longer have a hook to hang on.

Many more individual Germans, seeking the same civil and intellectual freedoms that motivated the Saxony Lutherans, followed them to settle the length of the river valley. By 1850, one of three citizens in St. Louis had been born in Germany. Joseph Pulitzer was one of St. Louis' German immigrants. The immigrants were active and successful in politics in St. Louis and thrived in villages along the Mississippi and Missouri rivers and in the foothills of the Ozarks.

According to Paul Nagel in *Missouri: A History*, both German immigrants and Yankees from the east brought anti-slavery viewpoints that generated great resentment among the locals with more southern leanings. By the 1850s, locals complained loudly that Missouri was becoming a home for anarchists and socialists. When anti-saloon marches began among the Baptists and Methodists, the German beer gardens were a prime target. During and after the Civil War, Missourians suffered long and deep for the attitudes of the southern white element in the state.

☼

Take Cty. A west out of Wittenberg through Frohna to Hwy. 61, then south to Jackson, 20 miles.

The village of **Frohna** is about half a mile from Altenburg. Frohna and Paitzdorf both have buildings restored from the 1830s. The **Saxon Lutheran Memorial** at Frohna is on the National Historic Register.

Jackson, Missouri

St. Louis Iron Mountain and Southern Railway ┏

Near Highway 61, five miles west of Cape Girardeau, 800-455-RAIL. Two cruises are offered: 1 1/2 hours or 2 hour dinner cruise. Call 800-455-RAIL. This is the area's only operating steam train and it dates back to 1858.

Bollinger Mill Historic Site
and Burford Covered Bridge

P.O. Box 248, Burfordville, MO 63739, 573-243-4591. National Register of Historic Places. Historic site, hiking, picnicking. Small fee.

The **Bollinger Mill** is a four-story brick mill with exhibits on milling. A 45-minute guided tour includes a demonstration of corn being ground into cornmeal between two millstones. A water-powered turbine provides the power to turn the runner (top) stone.

The **Burford Covered Bridge** is the oldest remaining covered bridge in Missouri, built between 1858 and 1868. The cover served mostly to protect the intricate structure of wood and iron from weather at a time when toll roads and bridges were privately operated. The bridge, which spans the Whitewater River, is 140 feet long with a clearance 14 feet high and 12 feet wide.

Burfordville Covered Bridge and Bollinger Mill State Historic Site.

To return to Illinois, continue south on U.S. Hwy. 61 to Cape Girardeau and cross the river on Hwy. 146. Or take I-55 to Sikeston and New Madrid. See Chapter 10 for Scott, New Madrid and Mississippi counties.

New Madrid, Mississippi &
Scott Counties, Missouri

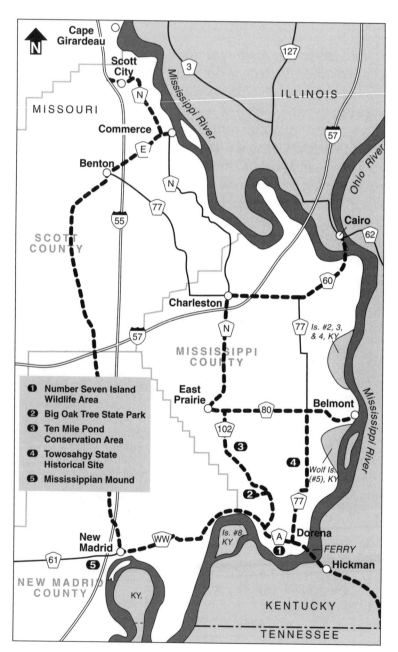

Cape Girardeau

Scott City

N

Scott COUNTY

MISSOURI

Commerce

E

Benton

55

77

N

N

3

Mississippi River

ILLINOIS

127

57

Ohio River

Cairo

62

60

Charleston

57

N

MISSISSIPPI COUNTY

77   Is. #2, 3, & 4, KY

❶ Number Seven Island Wildlife Area

❷ Big Oak Tree State Park

❸ Ten Mile Pond Conservation Area

❹ Towosahgy State Historical Site

❺ Mississippian Mound

East Prairie

80   Belmont

102

❸

❹   Wolf Is. (#5), KY

❷

77

New Madrid

WW   Is. #8, KY

61

❺

NEW MADRID COUNTY

KY.

A   Dorena

❶

FERRY

Hickman

KENTUCKY

TENNESSEE

Mississippi River

10

Scott, New Madrid &
Mississippi Counties, Missouri

Scott County, Missouri, south of Cape Girardeau, offers travelers a contrast between wooded hollows and overlooks in the Benton Hills (between Scott City and Benton) and table-flat fields of cotton, rice, corn and soybeans that stretch south from the base of the hills to Helena, Arkansas. The wet lowland plains of southeastern Missouri were formed when the ground sank during the earthquakes of 1811 and 1812.

The Little River Drainage System, which is the largest man-made lowland drainage system in the country, and a levee system that stretches for 1600 miles to south of New Orleans, protect this huge agricultural region from constant inundation by the river.

A BRIEF HISTORY OF SCOTT COUNTY

A state historical marker in front of the Scott County Courthouse in Benton relays much of the history of the county:

Scott County was the second county formed in Missouri's famed southeastern lowland region. It was organized in 1821 and named for the State's first congressman, John Scott. The first settlers were southerners who claimed Spanish land grants in the 1790s. The King's Highway was laid out in 1789 through territory claimed by the Osage Indians. By the 1820s, the Delaware lived in the area, displaced from their eastern lands. Benton was laid out in 1822, named for Thomas Hart Benton, one of Missouri's first U.S. Senators.

Commerce, laid out along the Mississippi River in 1823, was the first county seat, from 1864 to 1878. Long known as Tywappity, the settlement was a boat landing and trading post by 1790. There was formed the first Baptist church in what is now known as Missouri, in 1805. New Hamburg was the third town in the County, settled in the 1840s by German immigrants.

Sikeston was settled in 1800 and platted in 1860 by John Sikes, along the Cairo and Fulton Railroad.

The county, devastated by guerilla raids during the Civil War, grew rapidly from the 1870s to the early 1900s as its dense forests were lumbered off and drained for agriculture.

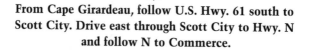

From Cape Girardeau, follow U.S. Hwy. 61 south to Scott City. Drive east through Scott City to Hwy. N and follow N to Commerce.

The drive to Commerce is exceptionally scenic, descending through the wooded hills and hollows of the Benton Hills. At Commerce the land again is table-flat.

Commerce, Missouri

Population 173

Only a few homes remain on the river's edge where Commerce has existed for nearly 200 years. The town is unprotected by a flood wall, and persistent high water in the 1990s finally prompted a voluntary government buyout of homes. Those who participated in the buyout generally moved farther up the hill or into nearby towns.

Those who choose to remain forfeit many rights to further government assistance if they rebuild in the flood plain, but many people have chosen to maintain a residence in or near Commerce—these are river lovers with a second home that is high and dry!

I visited with Joannie and Jerry Smith at their newly purchased riverfront home. We relished the balmy cool of a sunny fall day, watching the river bend sparkle as upbound tows stalled, giving way to boats running downstream through the big bend at Thebes Gap. Because boats traveling upstream are more maneuverable, those traveling downstream have right of way.

The grassy beach between the Smiths' sidewalk and the river is scheduled to become a Missouri Department of Natural Resources park with a boat ramp and picnic facilities, yet nearly every year, the river rises over the beach and licks at the Smiths' sidewalk. In bad flood years, like 1995, the water rises to the top of the five steps to the house.

Jerry is one of the new entrepreneurs who sees great opportunity in tiny riverfront towns offering a respite from the urban rush of St. Louis and Memphis.

"I'm betting my future, betting everything I have, on the economic potential of this village," he reminded me

Jerry Smith in his winery in Commerce.

more than once. "Look at this river view! Listen to the quiet! Its appeal will be irresistible for those living in large urban areas."

Jerry and his wife operate the River Ridge Winery and gift shop located in the scenic hills that back up against Commerce. Follow County Road 321 north from the riverfront for about 2 miles. You'll see the Anderson Guest House, built about 1848, presiding regally at the last corner before the road heads into the hills. Then the road becoms narrow, winding through very lovely rough country with narrow deep hollows. The winery, with its many outdoor tables, is set into one of these quiet, scenic hollows, and vineyards spread out of sight from the hilltop to the river.

———————————— ○ ————————————

Travel west from Commerce on County E to Benton, and then south on Hwy. 61 from Benton to Sikeston.

Sikeston, Missouri

Cotton is an important cash crop in the alluvial bottoms of southeast Missouri. Cotton bolls are picked mechanically and compacted in huge bins or trailers that are hauled straight to the cotton gin. "Ginning" includes cleaning the fibers, removing the seed, and compressing the clean cotton into 500-pound bales for sale to textile mills in South Carolina. The seeds are sold as cattle feed. There are cotton gins in both New Madrid and Caruthersville.

The **Sikeston Factory Outlet Stores** are just west of I-55 (exit #67) on Malone Ave., and several modern motels are clustered in the same area. Make reservations well in advance if you plan to arrive in August when the rodeo is in town. Sikeston is a good "hub city" for exploring southeastern Missouri. The **Klein House B&B** offers comfortable accomodations. For more accommodation information, call the Chamber of Commerce at 573-471-2498.

Lambert's Cafe, "home of the throwed rolls," is located about half a mile down the street from the Outlet Mall.

Outside Sikeston, a huge field of ready-to-pick cotton looks like a fresh snowfall on dry brown cotton plants. If you aren't thinking "cotton," the wisps of white stuff cluttering the streets of Sikeston look like litter!

There is always a long line outside the cafe; eating there is a memorable activity. Not only are hot rolls "throwed" to guests throughout the room, but servings come in huge skillets, side dishes like okra, hash browned potatoes, and sorghum are ladled out of huge kettles, and a serving of milk comes in a one-quart metal pitcher. When members of my family declined further servings, the waiter whispered to me confidentially, "Wimpy, ain't they!" No reservations. 573-471-4261.

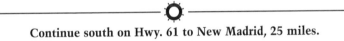

Continue south on Hwy. 61 to New Madrid, 25 miles.

New Madrid, Missouri
Population 3350

A BRIEF HISTORY OF NEW MADRID

As early as 1783, two French Canadian trappers and traders, François and Joseph LeSieur, set up camp on a bend of the river known as the Cove of Fat. In 1789, Col. George Morgan arrived to establish the City of New Madrid under a secret agreement with Spain. The original colony failed, but the name continues to this day.

The Civil War: When the Civil War began, New Madrid was culturally linked with the southern states, its settlers mainly from Kentucky, Virginia, and Tennessee and its agriculture-based society reliant on slave labor. General Pope's Union forces put the town to siege in early March, 1862, and Confederate forces withdrew to Island #10, just above New Madrid. In April, 1862, the Confederate forces at Island #10 surrendered. New Madrid's history, someone observed, more than that of many other towns, has been *shaped*—shaped by river, flood, earthquake, civil war, and by determined traders and farmers. (See pages 164 and 165 for more information about Island #10.)

WHAT TO SEE IN NEW MADRID

The New Madrid Historical Museum (A)

Monday through Saturday, 9 to 4 p.m. , Sunday noon to 4 p.m. From Memorial Day to Labor Day hours are extended to 5 p.m. 573-748-5944.

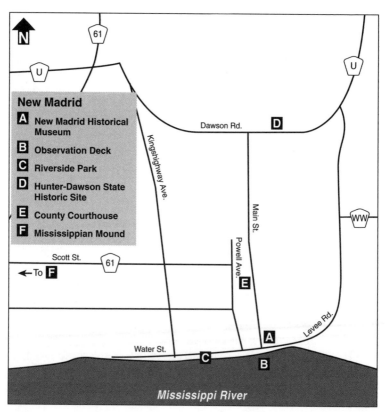

New Madrid

A New Madrid Historical Museum

B Observation Deck

C Riverside Park

D Hunter-Dawson State Historic Site

E County Courthouse

F Mississippian Mound

Here I learned about *sandboils*, which I later saw as large barren circles in the fields along the levee road from Dorena to Belmont. Sandboils occurred during the earthquake of 1811-12 and previous quakes when sand was forced to the surface by underground pressure. There is also an excellent do-it-yourself demonstration of *liquification*, which happens during earthquakes and floods when water rises up through sand, creating temporary quicksand. Anything sitting on the surface—including houses—will simply sink. The museum also has displays of artifacts from the Civil War and pioneer life and an excellent assortment of regional books.

The Mississippi River Observation Deck (B)

At the foot of Main Street.

The observation deck offers a panoramic view of the New Madrid Bend, a 20-mile-long oxbow. When you walk onto the 120-foot observation deck, look down on the supports of the right-hand side of the deck to find the water gauge. Often, (as in the photo below) there is not a drop of water until about 50 feet out from the gauge, but during 1995 and again in 1997, when both the Ohio and Mississippi Rivers were flooding, the river level reached nearly 43 feet.

The river before you in the oxbow flows west because of the double hairpin bend here. The large sandbar opposite is a public recreation area. During the 1840s, the orig-

Observation deck

INSIGHT

The New Madrid Earthquake of 1811-12

The first of three major earthquakes struck New Madrid and Little Prairie (south of New Madrid near modern-day Caruthersville) on December 16, 1811. It is believed to have been a magnitude of 8.6 on the Richter scale. A second quake, on January 23, 1812, was estimated to have been magnitude 8.4. The third quake, on February 7, may have been the strongest of the three and the most powerful to ever hit the North American continent, probably measuring 8.7 to 8.9 and releasing energy equivalent to 150,000,000 tons of TNT. In comparison, the combined energy of the two atomic bombs dropped on Hiroshima and Nagasaki in WWII equalled 35,000 to 40,000 tons of TNT.

When the tremors and convulsions of the earth subsided, 30 to 50 thousand square miles of land had undergone vast topographical changes, most of which are visible today. In the northwest corner of Tennessee, land dropped 10 to 20 feet and formed a lake we call Reelfoot (see page 195.) In places, the ground still shows the shape of the earthquake's undulating waves frozen into the compacted soil.

The New Madrid fault system extends 120 miles southward from the area of Charleston and Cairo through New Madrid and Caruthersville, following I-55 to Blytheville and on down to Marked Tree, Arkansas. Buried five to ten miles underground, it crosses five state lines and cuts across the Mississippi River in three places. The fault is active, averaging more than 300 measured events per year. Could another major earthquake occur in this area? Scientists suggest there is a 25% chance of a quake of 7.5 magnitude or more by the year 2040. A quake of this size would be felt throughout half the United Sates and cause damage in twenty states or more.

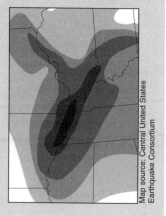

Estimated impact of a 7.0 to 7.3 earthquake along the New Madrid seismic zone

Map source: Central United States Earthquake Consortium

INSIGHT

Survivors of the Quake of 1811-1812

Witnesses report that about 2 a.m. on December 16, 1811, the earth around the little settlement of New Madrid began to rise and fall like waves upon the sea. When the peaks of the waves rolled through the Mississippi, the river bottom heaved up, emptying the river onto its banks, inundating the shores and leaving some boats on dry land. When the troughs followed, the river rushed back into the hollows with such force that entire groves of trees were drawn out by the roots and thrown into the river.

On dry land, trees bent like heads of grain in the wind, their branches interlocked, until they were ripped from the ground. Cracks formed in the earth that sometimes ran for miles. The quake's ground wave created sunken lands, fissures, and domes. *Sand blows* erupted sand and belched hot water, fumes, and carbonized wood.

Mattis M. Speed, a river traveler in February, 1812, described his experience: "We were awakened about 3 a.m. by the violent agitation of the boat accompanied by a noise so terrible it can best be described as the constant discharge of heavy cannon. The banks were falling into the river and the island to which we were tied was sinking. We cut ourselves loose from the island and pulled as far from the banks as necessary to avoid the falling trees. The swells of the river were so deep as to threaten the sinking of the boat every minute."

When he pulled out of the maelstrom at New Madrid, he wrote, "The former elevation of the bank was about 25 feet above common water. When we reached it, it was barely 12 or 13 feet. Scarcely a house was left entire, some completely prostrated, others unroofed and not a chimney standing."

One man described holding to a tree to support himself during a quake. A fissure opened in the ground and both he and the tree fell in. He was unable to climb out of the fissure at that point and was forced to walk along it until an incline allowed him to scramble out. Fissures as deep as 100 feet ran for miles through the countryside.

Source, in part, Reelfoot Lake and the New Madrid Fault *by Juanita Clifton as told to Lou Harshaw © 1980. Available at Reelfoot Lake Visitor Center or the New Madrid Museum.*

INSIGHT

A Brief History of Island #10 During the Civil War

The Confederates' first attempt to block the Mississippi was at Columbus, Kentucky. When General U.S. Grant chose instead to capture Fort Donnelson on the Tennessee River, he severed the supply line to Columbus and compelled the Confederates to abandon the site.

The next viable location lay 40 miles downstream at the hairpin double bends of the Mississippi near Island #10. At this point the river looks like an S laid on its side, with Island #10 at the bottom of its first bend and New Madrid at the top of the second bend. The island was considered crucial to the Union advance into the south.

In order for the Union to take Island #10, General Pope had to cut two supply routes: upstream by river, and by road leading from Tiptonville, Tennessee. By capturing New Madrid, Pope could bring the river under his guns and prevent any supply boats from reaching Island #10 from below.

Pope requested a run on the Confederate batteries at Island #10 by the ironclad gunboat fleet. Commander Foote refused him on the grounds of impracticality. Pope then appealed to Col. J. W. Bissel, who determined that a canal across the loop to New Madrid might be a possibility. Work began on March 19 and was accomplished within 16 days under bombardment. Six hundred engineers cut through underwater stumps with a sawing machine. The canal was 50 feet wide and 12 miles long, with 6 miles through heavy timber.

Continued on next page

inal village of New Madrid sat at what today is the Kentucky shore, on the other side of the sandbar. Today's Levee Road was then called Limit Street because it delineated the outer borders of the town. Notice how the river has fluctuated between 1862 and today by comparing the map of the New Madrid oxbow on the next page with the current shape on the map at the beginning of the chapter.

The two large smokestacks, which seem to lie south on

Because the river level dropped, the gunboats were unable to use the canal, although troop transports did pass through. Eventually, two Union gunboats ran the gauntlet past Island #10. With the link-up of transports and gunboats at New Madrid, General Pope could now cross the river.

On April 7, 1862, Union forces under General David Stanley crossed over to the Tennessee side. On the following morning, 5000 Confederate soldiers and Island #10, "key to the Mississippi Valley," were surrendered by General Wm. W. Mackall.

Author's Note: Thanks very much to Lynn Bock, a Civil War Historian from New Madrid for his help in verifying Civil War information throughout this volume.

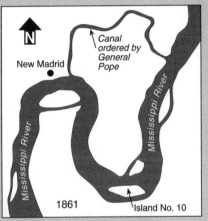

Notice how the river channel has changed since 1861. Island #10 is now part of the Missouri mainland. The shape of the New Madrid Bend is almost a perfect tear-drop shape with the neck less than one half a mile across. See current map at the beginning of the chapter.

the Tennessee shore, are actually in New Madrid's industrial park. One smokestack is from the power plant and one from the smelter at Noranda Aluminum, the largest employer in southeast Missouri with 1200 employees. Another large employer, the Louis Dreyfus Corporation, is the only rice mill in Missouri. Rice is a new crop for the area, with farmers taking advantage of abundant water in the easily irrigated lowlands.

Riverside Park (C)

Picnic tables, grills, alongside river just down from the observation deck.

Mississippian Indian Temple Mound (F)

This large mound is just south of the interchange of I-55 and U.S. Highway 61.

This is one of about 160 mounds that have been documented in the county. A diorama showing the way the village might have looked is displayed in the New Madrid Historical Museum.

Hunter-Dawson Home (D)

312 Dawson Road, 573-748-5340. $2 adults. $1.25 for children 6 to 12. Monday through Saturday 10 a.m. to 4 p.m., Sunday noon to 4 p.m.

This State Historic Site is an antebellum home of Greek-Revival Italianate style. It was planned by William Hunter, a wealthy Missouri gentleman, and completed by his wife Amanda after his premature death in 1859. Most of the furnishings displayed in the home belonged to her,

Hunter-Dawson Home

including one of the largest collections of Rammelsburg furniture in the country. Rammelsburg, noted for its distinctive carved designs, was made in Cincinnati during the 1860s. Note the walk-through windows off the formal living areas—walk-through windows were used because doors were taxable.

Robert Goah Watson, Amanda's father, was a Scottish-born fur trader who arrived in New Madrid before the earthquakes in 1811 and 1812. He stayed to rebuild when most settlers fled after the quakes. Young William Hunter had moved to New Madrid from Virginia to develop sawmills and gristmills. He worked for Robert Watson and eventually married Amanda. After Watson's death, Hunter turned the fur trade store into a general store and ran a steamboat selling dry goods in river towns. He also made loans, farmed, and sold and purchased property. The family owned 36 slaves and about 15,000 acres of land at the time of his death. General Pope's federal troops camped around the Hunter home during the siege of Island No. 10.

SPECIAL EVENTS IN NEW MADRID

For more information, contact City of New Madrid Department of Tourism, P.O. Box 96, New Madrid, MO 63869, phone 573-748-2866, fax 573-748-5402.

June 7: *Annual Heritage Craft Festival*

July 4: *Riverfront Festival*

September 19-20: *Arts/Crafts/Antique Fair*

Sept 17-21: *Riverboat Days*

December 13: *Hunter-Dawson Candlelight Tours* at Hunter-Dawson State Historic Site

---

To reach Mississippi County: From the Hunter-Dawson Home, turn left onto Dawson Rd., then right on Levee Rd. to State Route WW.

As you leave New Madrid County, Highway WW crosses **St. John's Bayou.** This is the last leg of Col. J.W. Bissel's canal and bayou route which bypassed Island No. 10, the Confederate stronghold, during the Civil War.

Mississippi County, Missouri

The state of Missouri claims more river frontage than any other state in the union, and aptly-named Mississippi County has more river frontage than any other county in the state, though the river itself is seldom visible to travelers. The county is known for its rich agricultural heritage and offers birders and naturalists a variety of terrains, from prairie to hardwood forest and swamp. Although the Great River Road doesn't pass through Mississippi County, the area is worth a visit if you avoid flood times, when its roads will be largely impassable. Its main attraction is the ferry to Hickman, Kentucky, and an opportunity to explore the back roads and natural areas of this wetland region.

Continue on WW. Turn north on 102.

WHAT TO SEE IN MISSISSIPPI COUNTY

Number Seven Island Wildlife Area ❶

At the intersection of 102 and A, just off the levee road.

Follow the gravel road over the levee into a backwater area replete with huge turtles and backwater birds. Named for the fact that the area was once Island # 7.

Big Oak Tree State Park ❷

Approximately 3 miles north of the intersection of WW and 102. Interpretive center, boardwalk, picnicking, fishing lake with small boat access and good fishing. No camping.

As you travel north on Highway 102, the park appears beyond flat fields of soybeans and corn as a strictly delineated section of old-growth trees. The soil of Mississippi

INSIGHT

River Island Numbering System

River islands were originally numbered south from the mouth of the Ohio in about 1805. Many islands no longer exist, as they have eroded or been incorporated into the mainland.

In some instances islands originally belonging to one state have been incorporated into the riverbanks of the state on the opposite shore. If this happens, to which state does that newly incorporated land belong? This is decided by how the land was acquired—suddenly or slowly. If acquired suddenly, as by flood or earthquake, the land remains under the jurisdiction of the original state. If it slowly migrates, or if the river channel slowly becomes so silted in that it joins the island with the opposite state, the land becomes a part of the new state.

County, enriched by eons of river flooding, produced unusually large trees—many that lived to be hundreds of years old. Persistent flooding, after vast acreages of land sank during the New Madrid earthquake, produced huge swamps throughout this section. Difficult access protected many of the old growth trees from loggers who were denuding Arkansas and Missouri after the Civil War.

Several champion trees are labeled in the picnic area and along walking trails. A *national* grand champion persimmon tree is behind the playground in the picnic area.

An excellent interpretive center and a boardwalk into the swampy bottomland forest are located just off the picnic area. Look for a guided tour booklet which may be available for the boardwalk. At station #1 is a canebrake and pawpaw trees. The protected Swainson's warbler requires cane for nesting, and this is one of only a few places where it is found in Missouri. At station #3, see a champion burr oak along the boardwalk—142 feet high and 17.7 inches in diameter.

The interpretive center is set on tall stilts. Yes, high water does reach right to the joists underneath! An excellent topographical model inside shows how the Ohio and Mississippi Rivers have wandered eastward from west of Crowley's Ridge and an ancient confluence at New Madrid. A display photo shows how the earthquake left impressions of ground waves still visible in the earth today.

The park road leads to a perfectly round, man-made fishing lake and a picnic area crowded with a few small cypress trees. The lake has small boat access and good fishing.

Continue north on 102 about 4 miles to
Ten Mile Pond Conservation Area.

Ten Mile Pond Conservation Area ❸

Marsh, waterfowl, public day use park.

American bald eagles, ducks, snow geese, and the closely related blue geese overwinter in the area.

From Ten Mile Pond, continue north toward Hwy. 80.
East Prairie is to the west of the 102/80 intersection and
Belmont is to the east. Charleston is north on Hwy. 105.

East Prairie, Missouri
Population 3416

East Prairie is located at the far eastern edge of a large prairie that stretches west toward Crowley's ridge, thus its name.

SPECIAL EVENTS IN THE EAST PRAIRIE AREA

September, third Saturday: *Living History Day.* Traditional arts and crafts. Big Oak Tree State Park.

October: *Fall Fest* in East Prairie

Mid-winter: *Winter's Wings Eagle Watch*, Ten Mile Pond Conservation Area

Belmont, Missouri

There was once a ferry here that carried travelers to Kentucky, but today the highway simply ends at the river. Belmont is the site of General Ulysses S. Grant's first Civil War skirmish—where Grant led his green troops to attack a small Confederate camp opposite the heavily armed fort on the bluffs of Columbus, Kentucky. In an effort to impede northern gunboats, Confederates had strung a chain—said to have been more than a mile long—across the river, securing it on the Columbus end with a huge anchor. The anchor and 65 feet of chain are displayed at the Columbus-Belmont State Park in Kentucky (see page 189).

———————— ⚙ ————————

From Belmont, you may return on Hwy. 80 as far as Hwy. 77 and then go north toward Charleston. Turn west on Hwy. 60 for the bridge to Cairo, Illinois.

Alternatively, take Hwy. 77 south to Dorena and board the toll ferry there to Hickman, Kentucky. If you're going south, the next opportunity to cross the river by *bridge* is at Caruthersville, near the southern border of Missouri. Along the way to Dorena, stop and visit Towosahgy State Historical Site.

Towosahgy State Historical Site ❹

Towosahgy is located south of Belmont and north of the Dorena ferry landing on Highway 77. This is an undeveloped 64-acre site with a small parking lot and a kiosk with interpretive exhibits.

Towosahgy is an Osage Indian word meaning "old town." This area was inhabited by Misssippian Indians from 1000 A.D. to 1400 A.D. and is believed to have contained about 73 homes, a central plaza, and a large ceremonial mound about 180 feet wide, 250 feet long and 16 feet high. The town was surrounded by a log stockade. Artifacts discovered in several pits included corn, beans, persimmon, wild plum and deer bones.

171

Today, it is a challenge to discern the remains of six mounds that surrounded the central plaza and the largest mound at the north end of the plaza.

Artist's conception of Towosahgy as it appeared 500 years ago.

Dorena, Missouri

The ferry landing at Dorena is a good spot for river watching. My own visit was rewarded by the sight of the steamboat *Delta Queen* passing by. It is best to estimate that the ferry will leave the Missouri shore on the hour, and that the last crossing to Kentucky will be an hour before dusk.

The Consolidated Grain and Barge Co. is right near the ferry landing and, in season, trucks will be hauling in corn or soybeans for loading onto barges. The company purchases the grain by the truckload, directly from the farmer, and ships the grain to an export elevator in new Orleans to be loaded onto ocean-going ships. Normally, the corn in this immediate area is some of the first to ripen in the United States, so it tends to command a premium price when shipped immediately. The soybeans might ripen a little late in the marketing cycle because of flooding, so it is often held in the elevators until the market is better.

Board the ferry and continue to Hickman, KY.

INSIGHT

John James Audubon

In 1806 a pair of French adventurers, Ferdinand Rozier and John James Audubon, traveled from Nantes, France, to trade in the New World. After trading for several years in Philadelphia and Kentucky, the pair brought 300 barrels of whiskey and other goods to Ste. Genevieve, Missouri. After a few weeks, Rozier dissolved the partnership to settle in Ste. Genevieve. Audubon returned to Kentucky. A milling venture there failed and the young man was literally forced into the life of an artist and ornithologist!

Audubon's comments about the keelboat trip are reproduced below as found in *The Story of Old Ste. Genevieve*, by Gregory Franzwa. The comments indicate that Audubon traveled much of the Missouri shoreline.

> After floating down the Ohio, we entered the Mississippi River running three miles an hour and bringing shoals of ice to further impede our progress. The patron ordered the line ashore, and it became the duty of every man "to haul the cordell," which was a rope fastened to the bow of the boat, and one man left on board to steer, the others laying the rope over their shoulders, slowly wafted the heavy boat and cargo against the current. We made seven miles that day ... At night we camped on the shores. Here we made fires, cooked supper and setting one sentinel, the rest went to bed ...
>
> Three more days of similar toil followed, when the weather became severe, and our patron ordered us to go into winter quarters, in the great bend of the Tawapatee Bottom [Commerce, Missouri!].
>
> There was not a white man's cabin within twenty miles, and that over a river we could not cross. We cut down trees and made a winter camp ... I rambled through the deep forests, and soon became acquainted with the Indian trails and the lakes in the neighborhood ...
>
> Here I passed six weeks pleasantly, investigating the habits of wild deer, bears, cougars, raccoons and turkeys, and many other animals, and I drew more or less by the side of our great campfire every day ... What a good fire it is ... Imagine four or five ash trees, three feet in diameter and sixty feet long cut, piled up, with all their limbs and branches, ten feet high, and then a fire kindled on the top with brush and dry leaves; and then under the smoke the party lies down and goes to sleep.

Western
Kentucky

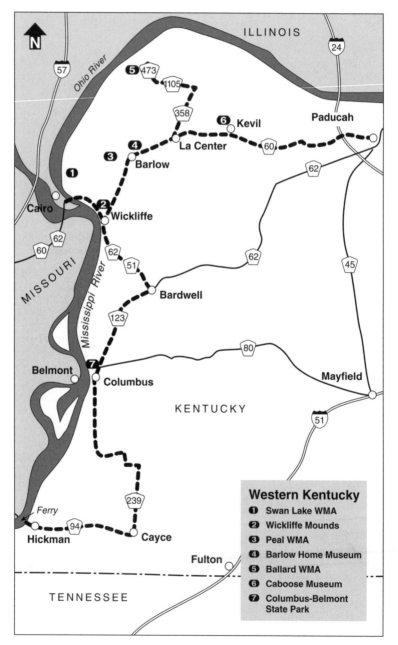

11

Western Kentucky

Ballard County, Kentucky

Our much-anticipated first crossing of the Ohio-Mississippi River confluence occurred during a gray, drizzly day in April. The Highway 51 bridge from Cairo was socked in by a fog bank so heavy that we were unable to see the river below, let alone wonder at the distinct blue-brown separation of the two rivers now flowing south side by side.

Here the "Upper" Mississippi becomes the "Lower" Mississippi. Silt and sediment from much of North America create the fertile soil of this northernmost portion of the Mississippi River Delta Region. You'll see no more locks and dams as you follow the Mississippi south because the bottomless silt, thousands of feet deep in places, provides no anchor for them. For the same reason, you'll see fewer bridges and find that the unstable river banks are often covered with concrete "mattresses" to slow erosion.

Under normal conditions, the Ohio River carries twice the volume of the Mississippi River, and during floods it may carry five times the volume of the Mississippi and Missouri Rivers combined! Sloughs, backwaters, and cypress swamps make the confluence of the Mississippi and Ohio Rivers a mecca for wintering waterfowl. There are several public wildlife management areas which offer hunting, fishing, camping, hiking and other amenities.

Major floodplain crops include corn, soybeans, and winter wheat. Tobacco, cattle and hogs contribute to the 30 million dollar agricultural business in Ballard county.

A BRIEF HISTORY OF BALLARD COUNTY

The namesake for this historic county in far Northwestern Kentucky was a frontiersman, Captain Bland Williams Ballard. His career parallels important historical times in the development of the American west: Ballard was born in Virginia in 1759. A hero of various Indian wars, he served five terms in the Kentucky legislature between 1795 and 1811. He fought at Tippecanoe, was wounded twice in the War of 1812 and escaped yet another Indian massacre. Ballard died in 1853, just shy of his hundredth birthday.

Ballard County, like so many counties in the border states, was occupied by Union soldiers during the Civil War. A Union encampment called Fort Jefferson was located about 5 miles south of Wickliffe, where today you'll find an historical marker on Highway 51. George Rogers Clark had established an earlier Fort Jefferson during 1780 and 1781 where Mayfield Creek empties into the Mississippi River. That location is believed to be buried under 16 to 20 feet of silt.

Suggested itinerary: Cross the bridge from Cairo and follow U.S. Hwy. 60 to Wickliffe, KY. On the way to Wickliffe, you may want to visit the Swan Lake Wildlife Management Area.

WHAT TO SEE IN BALLARD COUNTY

Swan Lake Wildlife Management Area ❶

This 2,536-acre area of bottomland and Ohio River floodplain is six miles northwest of Wickliffe on U.S. Highway 60. The area contains eleven lakes and six miles of gravel road. This is a superior site for waterfowl, including many nongame species such as songbirds, eagles, herons—and turtles.

The lakes in this area are surrounded by huge old cypress trees and offer excellent crappie and bluegill fishing. The largest of the lakes is Swan Lake. It was visited by John James Audubon in 1810 and named for the trumpeter swans that he and his Indian companions saw there. Today only the tundra swan is likely to be seen along the upper river during its late fall migration to the east coast. They are not seen this far south.

John James Audubon's tundra swan

Wickliffe Mounds ❷

On Highway 51-60 North at Wickliffe, 502-335-3681. Murray State University Research Center and Museum. There is a small fee for adults to tour the covered sites.

Here, atop a bluff overlooking the confluence of the Ohio and Mississippi rivers, an early Mississippian Indian village built its homes and ceremonial mounds. A ten-minute video at the Visitor Center and three covered excavation sites interpret the archeological excavation process that is currently taking place and the history of the mounds. Three buildings contain artifacts and features discovered in each area of the ancient village.

According to information from the Research Museum, the Mississippian village was active here for 250 years, between 1100 and 1350 A.D. The area that was once the site of villagers' homes is now covered by the **Lifeways Building**. Artifacts include pottery, grinding stones, post-hole patterns and evidence of infant burials. The **Ceme-**

tery Building displays information gathered from ancient burial sites. Studies provide information about life expectancy, infant mortality, evidence of disease and belief in an afterlife. Scientists do not yet understand the significance of the burial mounds and their alignments.

The **Architecture Building** shelters a platform mound built over a period of 200 years. The very first native building in this spot would have been built flat on the ground. As it aged or was destroyed, the mound building process was begun as another building was built on the foundation (platform) of the first. If sliced through the center, a platform mound would look very much like a layer cake. The largest mound is a ceremonial mound beside the Visitor Center. This particular mound was probably built in six different stages (or layers). Mounds are visible about every five to eight miles along the Great River Road. Most look like small rounded mounds in flat fields, but chances are that most were once large, flat-topped mounds.

Sketch of Mississippian Mounds from Illinois History of 1884.

An Archeological Weekend sponsored by the University each spring allows visitors to learn flint-knapping skills, how to use stone tools, make sandals, baskets, etc. Call 502-335-3681 for information. For a timeline of prehistoric cultures, see page 224.

———————————— ✷ ————————————

Continue east on Hwy. 60 to Barlow.

Barlow, Kentucky

WHAT TO SEE IN BARLOW

Peal Wildlife Management Area ❸   Λ ⌐

Peal Wildlife Management Area contains two tracts: Mitchell Tract is one mile west of Wickliffe on U.S. Highway 60, and the second tract is four miles west of Barlow on Holloway Landing Road. Primitive camping only on designated sites. No water or electrical hookups. Camping with recreational vehicles is not allowed in any of the Ballard County Wildlife Management Areas. These areas are closed from October 15 through March 15 and access to them is not allowed during times of high water.

The two tracts in Peal Wildlife Management Area contain 2,019 acres of marshland and river bottomland and three all-weather gravel roads, but no hiking trails.

Barlow Home Museum ❹   ⌐

Open Friday and Sunday through Monday, 1-4 p.m. Small fee.

During our April visit, the grounds of the Barlow Home Museum were alluring with tall flowering dogwood trees. The museum preserves the Barlows' Victorian family home and memorabilia collected since Thomas Jefferson Barlow founded the town in 1849.

———————————— ✷ ————————————

Continue on U.S. Hwy. 60 to La Center. To visit Ballard Wildlife Management Area, take KY 358, turn left on KY 1105 and right on KY 473.

Barlow Home Museum.

Ballard Wildlife Management Area ⑤

This 8,373-acre management area contains 20 miles of gravel roads around sloughs and agricultural bottomlands. River otter, bald and golden eagles are found in the area. When a pair of bald eagles nested in the area in 1986, it was the first active nest in Kentucky for over forty years!

Continue east on Hwy. 60 to Kevil and Paducah, a hub city for western Kentucky and the Land Between the Lakes recreational areas..

During our visit on a warm spring day, the countryside along Highway 60 was gorgeously green and rolling, and pink and white blossoming dogwoods and redbuds accented well-kept yards. This is the Kentucky we see in tourism brochures!

Caboose Museum ⑥

Open Sunday afternoons, free. Depicts history of Kevil.

Paducah, Kentucky

Population 26,000

Paducah thrives as the economic and cultural hub of western Kentucky. Many hotels and outlet malls line U.S. Highway 60, and many antique centers cluster in the historic old town. The **Museum of the American Quilter's Society** brings craftspeople from around the country, while the close proximity of the **Land Between the Lakes** means Paducah is also a recreational center. Besides the sites *in* Paducah, you may wish to visit the riverside Players Riverboat Casino in Metropolis, Illinois, on the opposite shore (I-24 west). Yes, this is *the* Metropolis, home of an annual Superman festival! You'll also want to check and see whether one of the great cruising steamboats of the Delta Queen Steamboat Company is docked at the Paducah levee.

As Paducah is located at the confluence of the Tennessee and Ohio Rivers, river-related businesses such as barge companies are very important to the area's economy. A

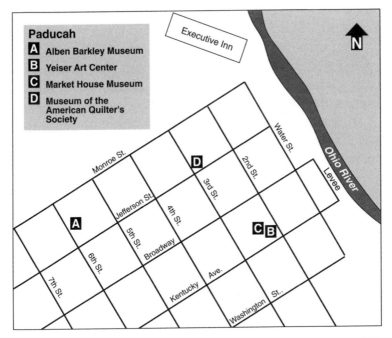

new multi-million-dollar River Center, at Water Street and Broadway, will open in 1998, combining the services of the Seamen's Church Institute and displays of river history and memorabilia at the **River Heritage Museum.** Visitors will have an unusual opportunity to watch seamen being trained in "brown water" (inland water) navigation as huge simulators recreate the process of "locking through" a lock and dam and other river challenges.

A BRIEF HISTORY OF PADUCAH

The town site dates from 1827 when William Clark purchased it for $5 from his brother, George Rogers Clark. It was established as the McCracken County Seat in 1832 and the First Market House was built of logs in 1836. The Second Market House was used as a Federal hospital during the Civil War. The current Market House, at 2nd and Broadway, was built in 1905 and is the home of the Market House Museum and the Yeiser Art Center. The town quickly became a successful commercial center, with steamboats, hotels, and farmers bringing in crops and stock. From 1870 to 1920, Paducah was second only to Louisville for commerce and manufacturing in the state.

Portions of the downtown area and the nearby lower town residential area are on the National Register of Historic Places, and there are many historical markers interpreting the history of McCracken County.

Dick Holland, local historian and author, notes that in the 1850s, a riverboat captain, who also worked for the telegraph company, figured that a telegraph cable could be insulated, coated with tar and run across the bottom of the river. He actually laid a cable beneath the Ohio River at Paducah to a telegraph station on the opposite shore. It worked for two weeks, just long enough for Cyrus West Field to study it, and in 1855 Field conceived the idea of laying a cable across the Atlantic. In 1858 the first message flashed across the ocean, but the very first underwater telegraph cable in the world was at Paducah.

PADUCAH IN THE CIVIL WAR

Paducah, very much a pro-South city, was nicknamed the "Charleston of the Jackson Purchase." Many early settlers came up the Tennessee and Cumberland Rivers with their slaves to settle the Jackson Purchase. As a result, one of General Grant's first moves in the Southern Campaign was to take possession of Paducah and to control the Ohio River, thus keeping Kentucky in the Union.

While Grant was only in Paducah one day before returning to Cairo, Illinois, the extended Union occupation was considered to be a "reign of terror" by local residents. One example of terrorism was an order from the Union commander that all Jewish merchants must leave the city. The merchants appealed the removal order to Abe Lincoln in a letter addressed to "Father Abraham." Legend has it that the removal order was so sudden and absolute that one merchant had no time to gather the cash he was counting, so he simply threw a newspaper over it. When allowed to return to the city, he found his store had been ransacked, but the newspaper still lay over his cash on the countertop.

General Grant's *Memoirs* realistically portray his dawn arrival at Paducah. He wrote, "I never saw such consternation depicted in the faces of the people. Men, women and children came out of the doors looking pale and frightened at the presence of the invader. They were expecting rebel troops that day."

"I assured them of our peaceful intentions ... evidently a relief to them; but the majority would have much preferred the presence of the other army."

WHAT TO SEE IN PADUCAH

If you are lucky enough to visit during the annual Dogwood Trail Festival, don't miss the opportunity to tour the blossom-bedecked neighborhoods. At night the blossoming trees and bushes are lit up with spotlights.

Whitehaven Kentucky Welcome Center

Exit # 7 off I-24. Free tours of the home are given from 1-4 p.m.

This beautifully restored white-columned ante-bellum home, operated by the state department of tourism, should be your first stop in Paducah. Whitehaven was the former home of U. S. Vice President Alben Barkley, who was sworn into office in 1949. It was abandoned in 1968 when the last family member left the home. During ensuing years, many of the original fixtures, including all of the stained glass, interior mirrors, doors and windows were either removed, stolen or damaged, and the house fell into disrepair. One could stand on the first floor and see the sky through gaping holes in the roof. During the home tour, notice woods that are "new" compared to the darker, original wood; it will give you an idea of how much of the home had to be rebuilt.

Alben Barkley Museum (A)

Madison and 6th Streets.

Yeiser Art Center (B)

In the Market Place building at 2nd Street and Broadway, 502-442-2453.

The Center contains displays of 19th & 20th-century American, Asian, European and African artworks. An international juried fiber show and arts display is always held during the Quilt Show in April and May.

Market House Museum (C)

The museum shares the Market House building with the Yeiser Art Center, 200 Broadway, 502-443-7759.

The Museum contains Indian and Civil War artifacts and a magnificent life-sized wood carving of an orator that was created by a 12-year-old boy whose family traveled downriver on a flatboat and carried the carving with them. It is believed to be based on a lithograph of Kentucky Senator Henry Clay giving a speech.

Curator Charles Manchester pointed out that the concrete floor slopes down from the center of the building for easy washing, as the museum was originally the butcher section of the Market Place. While you're at the Museum, ask to see the video documentary of the 1937 flood, when water in the downtown area reached the second floors of some buildings near the Market Place and rose 10 feet in the Market Place itself.

Located as Paducah is, at the confluence of the Ohio and Tennessee rivers, devastating floods have long been part of its heritage. The benchmark for modern floods is the Flood of 1937, when 16 days of continuous winter rain in

Mural of the Flood of 1937.

The Museum of the American Quilter's Society

Interview with Erik Reid

"The Museum of the American Quilter's Society grew from a nationwide quilt documentation project that began in Kentucky in the early 1980s. The original concern was that much of our state quilt history was being 'sold away' without documentation of the art. Quilts made in Kentucky and the Midwest sold for three times more on the East and West coasts than they did in Kentucky. All the best quilts were migrating out of the Midwest!

"The state's effort to photograph, document and collect native quilt art soon spread to thirty-four states. 'The Gatherings: America's Quilt Heritage Display' was the collection pulled from collections in each of the participating states.

"The first big quilt show was held in 1985 with cash awards of $25,000. Today nearly 40,000 visitors a year come to see both the quilt show and the many visiting collections that are displayed at the quilt museum. Thirty thousand visitors are in town during the American Quilt Show held each spring when over 400 quilts are on display at the Executive Inn convention hall. These visitors also attend workshops or lectures and visit approximately 100 merchants selling supplies, designs, and quilted items. More than $80,000 in cash is awarded during the Quilt Show and Contest.

"Here at the museum, we are a little liberal in our definition of quilts. Some of the quilt designers are known better in the art community than they are in the quilt community. Michael James, from Massachusetts, has developed a highly recognizable style over the past twenty years. Jan Meyer's expressive works often tell personal stories.

"Color, texture, pattern, and technique all enter into the art of quilt making. Quilt artists might be specialists in fabric dying or sculpture. We've even displayed a quilt done by a paper artist. It's made from paper, not fabric. As do most artists, quilt artists are always trying to push the limits.

"Caring for the collections is an art in itself. Different tex-

Continued on next page

Kentucky, Indiana, and Ohio produced three times the normal rainfall for the three states.

From January 17 through February 20, 1937, the river was above the flood stage of 43 feet, and the rivers wreaked havoc from Cincinnati to Paducah. Paducah was hardest hit, as it is not as high above sea level as cities farther up the river. It also received the full brunt of all the rivers that drain into the Ohio. Water covered Broadway all the way to 32nd Street. After the flood of 1937, a new Coca Cola bottling plant was constructed on 32nd Street and Broadway—the first dry ground above the rampaging Ohio River.

Museum of the American Quilter's Society (D)

3rd and Jefferson Streets. The Museum is normally open Tuesday through Saturday from 10 a.m. to 5 p.m., with hours extended during the annual quilt show. For further information concerning AQS membership or the AQS Quilt Show in late April, write to: AQS, P.O. Box 3290, Paducah, KY 42002-3290 (or call the museum at 502-442-8856).

The Museum has up to 150 quilts on display at any one time. During the Annual Quilt Show, over 400 quilts are displayed at the Executive Inn Conference Site, about six

tiles have different care techniques. One of our concerns is the light, which I'm adjusting today. Our flood lights have UV filters, but the lights need to be monitored just like you set the lighting for your camera. We try to keep the light at between 7 and 10 footcandles to keep the quilts from fading. At 5 p.m. the lights go off and don't come on again until 10 a.m. Fading is one reason we don't allow flash photography inside the museum.

"We've had quilts displayed from more than ten countries, including collections from Russia and Japan. We have the largest display of amateur and professional quilts in the world, and visitors come from all over the world to see quilt designs as varied as the countries they represent. In fact, my favorite quilt quote is, 'You can't make a blanket statement about quilters, because they are so diverse!'"

blocks west of Broadway on the waterfront. During our visit, we were assured that the displays would be of interest to the whole family—Dad and kids included, but we still were not prepared for the fascinating variety of textile arts which adorned the walls of the museum. Erik Reid, assistant curator at the time, was carefully adjusting levels of display lights when I asked him to explain a little about the museum and the artists displayed there (see previous pages).

SPECIAL EVENTS IN PADUCAH

Mid-April: *Paducah Dogwood Trail Celebration.* Enjoy the beauty of dogwood blossoms in a lighted 12-mile trail. Festival of the Arts features music, theater, flower and art shows. 800-PADUCAH.

Late April: *American Quilter's Society National Show and Contest.* More than 400 quilts and wall hangings are exhibited. Several quilt-related events are held throughout the city, including the Fantastic Fibers exhibit at the Yeiser Art Center. 502-898-7903.

Early June: *Paducah's Festival of Murals.* Living History performances, music, food, and book signings by regional authors. Concert by the Paducah Symphony, catered dinners, and featured artists. 502-444-0065.

Mid-July: *Paducah Summer Festival* on the Ohio Riverfront. Bicycle Stage Race is sanctioned by U.S. Cycling Federation. Call 502-442-0751. Also, cross-river swim, hot air balloons, sky divers, fireworks, arts and crafts, musical entertainment. 800-PADUCAH.

Mid-September: *Antique Gas & Steam Engine Show* in Carson Park. Features antique cars, tractors and engines. Tractor pulls, wheat threshing, pulling teams, arts & crafts, barbecues. 502-444-8649.

Late September: *Old Market Days & Barbecue* on the River. Popular barbecue competition, crafts, collectibles, sidewalk sales, demonstrations and games.

Market House Square, Second Street between Broadway and Kentucky Ave., 800-PADUCAH.

ACCOMMODATIONS IN PADUCAH
For hotel information, contact the Paducah-McCracken County Convention and Visitors Bureau at 128 Broadway, Paducah, KY 42001. 800-359-4775.

———————— **✸** ————————

To continue on Kentucky's Great River Road, return to Wickliffe on Hwy. 60, and then south to Bardwell. Alternatively, take Hwy. 62 from Paducah to Bardwell. In either case, continue south from Bardwell on Rte. 123 to Columbus, the site of Columbus-Belmont State Park.

To omit the visit to Columbus-Belmont State Park and continue straight to Tennessee, take Hwy. 45 south to Mayfield, Fulton, and then on to Union City, TN.

Columbus, Kentucky

Columbus-Belmont State Park ❼   ▲ 👫 🚩

156 acre park 15 miles south of Wickliffe Mounds at KY-58 & KY-123/80, 502-677-2327. Museum (May through Labor Day, 9 to 5, April and Labor Day through October, open Saturday and Sunday), mini-golf, hiking, year-round camping.

This is a favorite Civil War site for many who travel the Great River Road. On display are the massive chain and anchor that lay draped between Belmont and Columbus to block the passage of Union gunboats during the Civil War, and a network of earthen trenches is still visible. Confederate cannons fired from the fort here broke up Grant's skirmish at Belmont, Missouri. Eventually, Grant's troops flanked the outpost and it was abandoned.

Many area families still have souvenir cannonballs or bullets found in the fields between Columbus and Tiptonville, Tennessee.

Major Civil War Battles Fought Above Vicksburg, Mississippi

- **November 7, 1861**—U.S. Grant leads green troops into battle at Belmont, Missouri.

- **March 14, 1862** Confederates abandon New Madrid, Missouri.

- **April 7-8, 1862**—Battle of Shiloh.

- **April 8, 1862**—Island #10 captured by Union General John Pope. 5,000 Confederate soldiers captured.

- **June 4, 1862**—Confederates evacuate Fort Pillow, Tennessee.

- **June 6, 1862**—Union soldiers occupy Memphis, Tennessee, after a brief naval battle.

- **January 10-11, 1863**—Arkansas Post surrenders, 5000 Confederates captured.

- **May 18, 1863**—Grant begins the siege of Vicksburg, Mississippi.

**Continue south on Hwys. 123 and 239
for 18 miles to Cayce.**

Cayce, Kentucky

John Luther Jones, 1864-1900, was a celebrated American locomotive engineer born in Fulton County, Kentucky, and nicknamed for Cayce, Kentucky, where he worked. When driving the Cannon Ball express from Memphis, Tennessee, to Canton, Mississippi, he applied the brakes in time to save the lives of the passengers in a wreck at Vaughan, Mississippi. Only Casey Jones died in the wreck. Casey's home has been moved to the **Old Country Store** in Cayce, a shopping complex designed to resemble a turn-of-the century Main Street. There are also displays of his personal articles and train memorabilia.

Continue west on Hwy. 94 for 9 miles to Hickman.

Hickman, Kentucky

This blufftop community includes many beautiful Victorian homes overlooking the river on Clinton Street. Eroding bluffs threaten many of the homes as well as the Fulton County Courthouse built in 1903. Hickman, a port for agricultural products, has the only still water harbor between St. Louis and Memphis, offering boats shelter from the relentless current and occasional floating ice in the main river.

The ferry that crosses the river from Dorena to Hickman has operated nearly continuously for over 150 years. The nearest river bridges are 50 miles north at Cairo, Illinois, and 50 miles south at Dyersburg, Tennessee and Caruthersville, Missouri.

As you leave Kentucky, notice the New Madrid Bend, "Kentucky's Forgotten Territory," on your road map. Located just opposite New Madrid, Missouri, it contains 12,000 acres of America's most fertile soil. This bit of Kentucky is accessible only by a road from Tennessee! See page 169 for information on how islands along the Mississippi often migrate from state to state.

Continue south on Hwy. 94, which changes to Hwy. 78 as you cross the Kentucky/Tennessee state line and head for Reelfoot Lake. If you are arriving from Fulton, continue to Union City, the starting point for Chapter 12.

Western
Tennessee

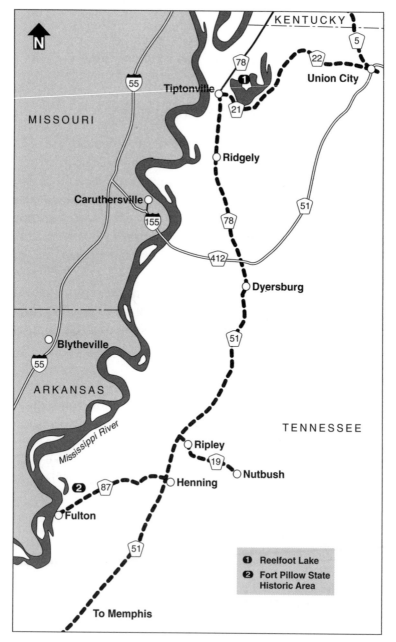

12

Western Tennessee

Western Tennessee and Kentucky contain many of the most rural stretches along the Great River Road. Memphis, Tennessee, is the only large city along the roadway in these two states, but there are other sights to see: **Reelfoot Lake State Park and Resort**, in northwestern Tennessee, offers an outstanding natural attraction just off the Mississippi River, and **Fort Pillow State Historic Site**, just north of Memphis, is the well-preserved site of a controversial Civil War battle.

HISTORY: THE JACKSON PURCHASE

References to "The Purchase" appear frequently as part of place and road names in western Kentucky and Tennessee. According to Ron Satz, author of *Tennessee's Indian People*, Andrew Jackson and Isaac Shelby, a former governor of Kentucky, were commissioned by North Carolina to negotiate with the Chickasaw Indians for the cession of Indian lands in western Tennessee and Kentucky. The resulting Jackson Purchase in October of 1818 extinguished Indian rights to about 10,700 square miles.

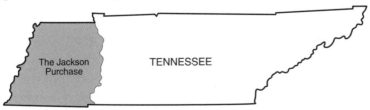

The Purchase allowed the Chickasaw Indians $15,000 a year for twenty years—or about five cents an acre for six million acres. A few months after the Purchase was finalized, the town of Memphis was laid out on the Lower Chickasaw Bluffs, and by 1838, General Andrew Jackson had authorized the removal of the entire Indian population to Oklahoma.

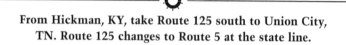

From Hickman, KY, take Route 125 south to Union City, TN. Route 125 changes to Route 5 at the state line.

Union City, Tennessee

Union City is the county seat of Obion County (pronounced *o-bine*), one of the top pork-producing counties in Tennessee, so this is the place to try a salt-cured Tennessee country ham. During the Civil War, the 1,000 citizens of Union City quartered between 5,000 and 20,000 Confederate soldiers, and Union City was the first city in Tennessee to erect a monument to the unknown Confederate soldier.

Settlers began homesteading Obion County in about 1819. Most small towns in the Tennessee floodplain were established in the years before the Civil War as steamboats and the new steam train engines brought in streams of white settlers.

Davy Crockett (1786-1836) lived just south of Union City, near Greenville, Tennessee. He served as Tennessee's U.S. Representative from 1827 to 1831 and 1833 to 1835, and died defending the Alamo in Texas.

GEOLOGY: THE LOESS HILLS

The rich soil found on the hills near Union City is composed of dried glacial debris ("loess") deposited by winds during the last ice age. The glacier to the north and warm seas to the south created huge temperature differences that resulted in fierce winds and immense dust storms blowing in from the northwest. Loess here is about 80 feet thick.

———————————— ✺ ————————————

Follow Highway 22 west from Union City to Reelfoot Lake. Approximate mileage from Reelfoot Lake: Union City, 28 miles; Dyersburg, TN, 30 miles; St. Louis, 200 miles; Chicago, 475 miles, Indianapolis, 420 miles; Nashville, 200 miles; Memphis 100 miles.

Reelfoot Lake State Park

State Hwy. 21/Route 1, Tiptonville, TN 38079, 901-253-7756. Reelfoot Lake Tourism office is at the junction of Hwys. 21 and 22. P.O. Box 9, Dept. K-V, Samburg, TN 38254, 901-538-2666.

This is one of Tennessee's popular resort parks. The state-operated Airpark Inn Resort and Restaurant are built over the lake among bald cypress trees. Adjacent to the Inn is an all-weather, 3,500-foot, lighted airstrip. The park offers camping, picnicking, and an excellent visitor center.

We found Reelfoot Lake State Park in April to be memorable for its natural beauty. Bald cypress trees soaked in the water and turtles lined up on an algae-lapped log in the swamp. Ovenbirds called "teacher, teacher, teacher, teach!" A full moon reflected on a silvery lake steeped in silence, broken only by the periodic "Thump" of a bullfrog, the squawk of a great blue heron and the slap of spawning crappies.

Turtles lined up on a log.

195

WHAT TO SEE AND DO AT REELFOOT LAKE

Kirby Pocket Day Use Area (A)

Boat launch, picnic tables.

Acres of bald knob cypress surrounded by "knees" remind us that Reelfoot is truly a southern lake. The huge molded plastic fish in the picnic area are models of crappies.

South End Campground (B)

Open April 1 to October 31. Electricity, water. No reservations.

Large seasonal state park camping area at the base of the lake. Tall cypress, sweet gum, tulip poplars, cotton-woods, oaks and maples provide abundant shade.

Spillway Day Use Area (C)

Picnicking, boat rentals, State Park Motel, bait shop.

Blue Bank Day Use Area (D)

This area is crowded with bald cypress. It was originally called Crockett's Pasture for a son-in-law of Tennessee's legendary Davy Crockett, and a nearby Methodist Church is named Crockett's Chapel. Campers often came in horse-pulled wagons or buggies to set up camp on the high ground, purchasing hay locally for use as camp bedding.

Two cafes near the Blue Bank area, the Lakeview Dining Room and the Blue Bank Dining Room and Motel, offer fresh lake crappie in season (October 15-March 15).

Kiwanis Day Use Area   ⅊

Public fishing pier, miniature golf, and various kiddy rides. This privately-run picnicking and recreation area is open seasonally.

Reelfoot Lake Visitor Center (E)   ⅊ ⻍ ⛰

Picnicking, nature walks, displays.

Plan to explore the edge of Reelfoot Lake on the boardwalk here among the cypress. Unreleasable raptors (disabled eagles, hawks, and owls) are caged outside the Center for easy viewing by the public, and there are excellent interpretive displays inside.

Giant crappies decorate the grounds of Kirby Pocket Day Use Area.

197

New Madrid Earthquake Creates Reelfoot Lake

Both Reelfoot Lake and St. Francis Lake in Arkansas were formed by the New Madrid Earthquake in 1811-12. A citizen from New Madrid, Missouri, wrote in 1816, "Lately, it has been discovered that a Lake was formed on the opposite side of the Mississippi, in the Indian country, upwards of 100 miles long and from one to six miles wide, of a depth of from 10 to 50 feet."

The epicenter of the quake was about 70 miles southwest of modern Reelfoot Lake and more than 1800 recorded tremors, some of which rang bells on the east coast, followed the first powerful jolt.

In 1815 Congress passed an act to relieve area inhabitants who found their riverside farms swallowed up or buried in the sand that spewed from the earth. More than 500 earthquake certificates, redeemable for up to 640 acres of government land, were allotted. The site of Hannibal, Missouri, was one of those land grants.

TIPTONVILLE DOME

A dome-like rise in the otherwise perfectly flat land is clearly visible on the west side of the lake, on the road from the Airpark Inn to Tiptonville. The Tiptonville Dome formed when the land around Reelfoot Lake sank during the earthquake. Above the newly-formed depression, the Mississippi River appeared to flow backward when the waters rushed to fill the depression—the center of which is now Reelfoot Lake.

The raising of the dome also created a natural dam that, for a short time, forced the river to flow back south upon itself. The same dam trapped water in low swampland in the vicinity of Reelfoot Creek and Bayou de Chien, eventually allowing Reelfoot Lake to form.

For more information about the New Madrid Earthquake,
see page 162.

Bald Eagle Tours   ⚓

Daily from December to mid-March. Advance registration required, 901-253-7756.

Five to seven thousand visitors participate in tours during this short season, hence the requirement for advance registration! See pages 200-201 for more about the eagle population.

Pontoon Lake Tours   ⚓

May 1 to October 1. Three-hour tour includes a rest stop at the Caney Island Indian mounds. Bring your own soft drinks and snacks.

From the end of May through August, the waterlilies on the lake are in full bloom. The park offers a daily pontoon boat cruise, highly recommended, which makes lily-viewing easy. You'll see American lilies with yellow flowers up to a foot across, fragrant lilies with white flowers, purple pickerelweed, and spatterdock—a yellow golf-ball-shaped lily.

The Reelfoot Lake Boat

This unique craft is manufactured at Calhoun Boat Works across from the Visitor Center. It's a cross between a johnboat and a canoe, and its inboard motor is specially protected from cypress stumps and knees. Reelfoot Lake boats can be rented locally.

North End RV Camp (F)   **⛺**

Fourteen sites with water and electricity; some primitive camping is available.

This camp is directly opposite the Airpark Inn Resort and is open year-round.

Airpark Inn Resort (G)   ⚓

Townhouse accommodations, airstrip, tennis courts, swimming pool, restaurant, weekend packages, nature trail. Buffet meals at the Resort are reasonably priced. Special weekend packages

INSIGHT

Nightriders at Reelfoot Lake

According to displays at the Visitor Center, Nightrider activity around Reelfoot Lake reflected conflict between the local settlers, who struggled to make a living by hunting and fishing around the lake, and big money interests who bought the lake in the nineteenth century, intending to drain it for agricultural use.

The Nightriders organized at first to harass the lake owners and defend their right to make a living, but after the Civil War they became a vigilante group. Wearing masks of meal sacks and gowns of calico or bed quilts, members took it upon themselves to instill their brand of morality and citizenship upon all settlers in the area. In 1914, six Nightriders were sentenced to hang for murder and attempted murder. Shortely afterwards, the lake was placed in the public domain and the Nightrider phenomenon disappeared.

are available for parties of two and for families of four (includes 3 nights, 4 dinners, and 4 breakfasts).

As you walk to the Resort lobby from the parking lot, look for "eagle snags" — bare, isolated, branches in a tall bald cypress to the right. During the eagle watching season,

there are almost always two eagles sitting there—probably the most photographed eagles in Tennessee! Eagles will commandeer individual branches and return to them each year.

A nature trail from the resort parking lot allows an easy walk along the swampy lake edge among the huge bald cypress.

INSIGHT

Wildlife Watching
in the Reelfoot Lake Area

There are at least 250 species of birds in the park, 11 species of turtle, 54 of fish, and 24 of snakes.

BIRDS

Peak bird migration is from April to mid-May. Look for shorebirds, wetland species, waterfowl and 150 species of songbirds. The heron rookery at Reelfoot Lake has recovered from a decline caused by boat traffic and pesticides in the 1950s to number nearly 2000 birds today.

Reelfoot Lake claims one of the highest concentrations of American bald eagles east of the Mississippi River. The term "bald" actually refers to the eagle's white head—white is "balde" in old English. Males in this area are 6 to 9 pounds, females are 20% to 30% larger. On the upper river, females may reach 16 pounds.

The eagles' diet is 80% to 90% fish plus a few rabbits and ducks. They mate for life but will remate if a mate dies. Their nests are about five feet wide. The young fledge at 10 to 12 weeks and are sexually mature at four to five years.

From 1920 to 1930, market hunters shipped trainloads of ducks to Chicago from Reelfoot Lake. It is believed that a record 2800 were bagged on one day in the 1920s. Canvasbacks were worth one dollar, mallards fifty cents.

FISH

Reelfoot's shallow, fertile waters and the abundance of natural cover make it one of the world's finest natural fish hatcheries. Fifty-four species of fish live in the lake, including bream, several species of catfish, white and black crappie, and largemouth and yellow bass.

Numerous guides and fishing camps around the lake are listed in a handout available at the Reelfoot Lake Tourism office, and private resorts, bait shops, and hunting/fishing guides are advertised along the road encircling the lake.

Continued on next page

The main public fishing seasons are March through July and September through October. There is no daily limit, and a catch of 100 or more crappie is possible.

Reelfoot is the only lake in the United States that allows commercial harvesting of a game fish. In the late 1800s, commercial fishermen shipped their abundant catch to New York where catfish brought $.23 per pound. The eggs were sold for caviar. The men worked at night, attracting fish to the boat with the light of a fire in a metal hoop extended over the water. Trotlines were set from stump to stump. In the morning they returned to the dock with 200 to 2000 pounds of fish in the boat.

What's the Name of This Fish??

The bowfin, often caught in Reelfoot Lake, has left many a fisherman scratching his head wondering what kind of creature he found at the end of his line. One fisherman described his 24-inch specimen as a catfish with big teeth and an extremely strong fighter. Bowfin feed almost exclusively on other fish and are not considered edible by fishermen.

The bowfin is the only remaining representative of a family of fish dating back 180 million years. They still have a "swim bladder" that allows them to breathe air, and they can live in stagnant water that would kill most other fish.

Gar, bowfin, paddlefish, and sturgeon—some of the oddest looking fish in the Mississippi River—are also among the oldest freshwater species in existence. The north-south orientation of the river meant that during glacial periods, fish could retreat to the lower river and return when river temperatures were more hospitable.

SNAKES

Venomous cottonmouths and canebrake rattlers live in the Reelfoot Lake area but are seldom seen. The general rule is, leave them alone and they will leave you alone. From May to June, however, all snakes are more aggressive and more likely to be seen. During this time they will sometimes strike without warning, and even the rattlers may not rattle a warning. Use a stick, not your hands, when disturbing leaves or other forest debris.

Park Host Riley Sullivan told me that as a boy, he and his friends would sometimes find snake dens in the spring. The dens were secluded and sheltered and as big as a large room, with snakes hanging from and coiling around rocks and fallen logs. Dozens of snakes sometimes intertwined into balls as big as a man's arm.

"Us boys would swing on a grape vine over these balls of snakes, trying to rile the snakes into striking," Riley related. "The goal was to see how close you could kick at an angry snake without getting bit."

" 'Course, I wouldn't do that now for nuthin'," he told me, "but we lived in the country down along the banks of the river and that was our form of recreation—a chance for us boys to show how tough we were. What really happened was that by the time the snake reacted to our kick and struck, we had already swung out of reach. I don't know why they didn't get us on the way back, but they didn't, and nobody ever got bit."

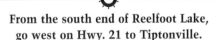

From the south end of Reelfoot Lake,
go west on Hwy. 21 to Tiptonville.

Tiptonville, Tennessee
Population 2800

Most of the earliest white settlers in this area migrated from the Carolinas and were of Scotch, Irish, or English descent. Many were involved with timber sales and commercial hunting and fishing. Huge plantations were developed on the high dome formed by the earthquake and produced cotton, winter wheat, soybeans and corn.

King Cotton: Agriculture in the Delta

The well-drained, sandy loam of the Mississippi River delta in Lake County (where Tiptonville and Reelfoot Lake are located) has been enriched by years of deposits from the flooding Mississippi and continual erosion of loess from the surrounding hills. The land is perfectly flat, with variation in sea level of not more than 10 feet. Farmers alternate between crops of winter wheat, soybeans, corn and a rich cotton crop. The fertile land is valued at $6000 to $8000 an acre.

Very little cotton was grown in the area until after the Civil War. In 1865, W. E. Batsell installed the first cotton gin, and by the 1950s, this area produced more cotton bales per acre than anyplace in the United States.

Even today, a lot of handwork is involved in caring for the cotton crop, though the use of chemicals has reduced the hours of hoeing and weeding required. Crews still "chop" (or hoe) the cotton for two or three months—up through August—and as recently as the early 1960s schools let out for two weeks in October so kids could handpick cotton in the fields. But by 1962 to 1964, most farms had switched over to cotton picking machines.

According to Helen at the Phoenix Cotton Gin in Tiptonville, "While this area is rich delta cotton country and the old plantations were huge, we really did not have many of the big antebellum-type homes found further to the south. One family might have owned all the land from Reelfoot Lake to the Mississippi River ... They could ride their horses from one to the other on their own land. The price for cotton now is higher than it was in 1865—over $1 a pound in special markets and about 79 cents per pound in general. More cotton is being planted as a result."

A tractor pulls a bale of cotton in Tiptonville.

The present community is named for William Tipton, who founded the town in 1857. It developed as a shipping and receiving point for river traffic, but its early years were traumatic since the entire area of Tiptonville and Island #10 were under siege from Union soldiers during the spring of 1862.

Union forces set up cannons on the Missouri shore opposite Tiptonville and pounded the area with cannonballs. Cannon fire was followed by the arrival of federal ironclad gunboats, which helped to assure serious damage to every business and most residences in the town. On April 8, 1862, the Confederates surrendered and the area was held by the Union for the duration of the war. To this day cannonballs are found in the fields and nearly every family has one.

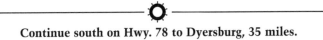

Continue south on Hwy. 78 to Dyersburg, 35 miles.

Dyersburg, Tennessee
Population 21,000
Dyers County Chamber of Commerce, 901-285-3433.

The county seat for Dyer County is a prosperous, well-kept community, where dogwood, redbud, and azaleas bloom in April. The county was named for Joel H. Dyer, owner of the land grant for the town. Road signs identify Key Corner, the point from which Henry Rutherford began, in 1783, to survey North Carolina land grants, most of which contained 5,000 acres.

Across the river is Caruthersville, Missouri, founded as *Petit Prairie* (Little Prairie) by Francois Le Sieur, who also founded New Madrid, Missouri. After the earthquake in 1811-12, only two families remained in Caruthersville.

Forty-five years later, Petit Prairie was replatted and named for Representative Sam Caruthers, who aided in the establishment of the town. It was named the new county seat. Today, with the help of levees and modern drainage techniques, Pemiscot County, Missouri, is one of the most fertile farming areas in the nation.

WHAT TO SEE IN DYERSBURG

Dr. Walter E. David Wildlife Museum

This museum contains specimens of every duck species on the Mississippi Flyway. Located on the campus of Dyersburg State Community College.

Casino Aztar

777 East Third, on the Mississippi River in downtown Caruthersville, Missouri, 573-333-1000.

Enjoy riverboat gambling and visit the nearby Expo Center for concerts, art/craft show, rodeo arena and other entertainment.

───────────── ✵ ─────────────

Continue south toward Memphis on Hwy. 51.

On the Road to Memphis

Twenty-five miles south of Dyersburg is Ripley. An eight-mile side trip east on Highway 19 takes you to **Nutbush**, the girlhood home of singer Tina Turner (Annie Mae Bullocks), where you can tour Turner's birthplace and the Nutbush Heritage Exhibit. **Henning**, 5 miles south of Ripley on Highway 51, is the boyhood home of Alex Haley, Pulitzer Prize-winning author of *Roots*. 901-738-2240.

───────────── ✵ ─────────────

Turn off U.S. Hwy. 51 at Henning and travel west on Hwy. 87 for 20 miles to the village of Fulton and the Fort Pillow State Historic Area north of town.

Fulton and the Fort Pillow State Historic Area

WHAT TO SEE IN THE FORT PILLOW AREA

Fort Pillow State Historic Area   ⚐⚐ ∆ ⚑

Route 2, Box 108 B-1, Henning, TN, 901-738-5581.

The 1,646-acre park is located on the Chickasaw Bluffs overlooking the Mississippi River. In 1861, the Confederate army built extensive fortifications here and named the site for General Gideon J. Pillow. The fort was overrun by the Union army, which controlled it during most of the war. One of the war's most controversial battles occurred when Confederate troops retook the fort, which was defended by mostly black Union troops. For years, both sides debated whether Confederate forces had been unecessarily brutal to black defenders. Remains of the fort's earthworks are well preserved.

This is a rich birding and wildlife area, with scenic Cold Creek flowing into a bottomland hardwood slough.

Hatchie State Scenic River
and Chickasaw Wildlife Refuge   ⚑ ⚏ ∆ ⛴

Route 2, Box 109 A, Henning, TN 38041. Interpretive center, camping, gift shop, picnicking, boat launch. 901-738-5581

— ☼ —

Continue south on Hwy. 51 until the intersection with I-40. From the north, take I-40 into Memphis, exit west at Madison, turn left on Dunlap and follow Union Avenue to the large hotels (Peabody, Radisson, and Ramada) a few blocks from the Memphis riverfront. Beale Street is right there, too, as are the horse carriages and easy access to freeways for visiting other areas of town.

Memphis,
Tennessee

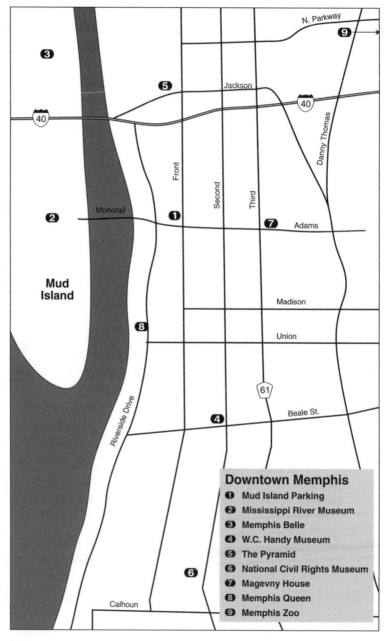

N. Parkway

❾

❸

❺   Jackson

🛡40

🛡40

Danny Thomas

Front

Second

Third

Monorail

❷   ❶   ❼   Adams

Mud
Island

Madison

❽

Union

🛡61

❹   Beale St.

Riverside Drive

Downtown Memphis

❶   Mud Island Parking
❷   Mississippi River Museum
❸   Memphis Belle
❹   W.C. Handy Museum
❺   The Pyramid
❻   National Civil Rights Museum
❼   Magevny House
❽   Memphis Queen
❾   Memphis Zoo

❻

Calhoun

13

Memphis Area

Memphis, Tennessee
Population 614,289

Memphis delighted our whole family with its pleasant, manageable layout and varied attractions. It is the county seat for Shelby County and the largest city in Tennessee. It has long been a major river port, rail center, and market for lumber, cotton, and livestock. Strategically important during the Civil War, it fell to the Union in 1862. **St. Jude's Hospital** and Elvis Presley's home, **Graceland**, are here. **Martin Luther King** was assassinated at the Lorraine Motel in 1968.

Our Ramada Inn was ideally located for easy sightseeing. We visited the Peabody Hotel with its elegant lounge and resident ducks and took the elevator to the roof and enjoyed the music rising up from Beale Street, a block away.

For more Memphis accommodations and a complete list of its many special events and attractions, contact the Memphis Convention and Visitors Bureau at 47 Union Avenue, Memphis, 901-543-5300 or visit their web site at http://www.memphis travel.com

A BRIEF HISTORY OF MEMPHIS
Memphis, located at the mouth of the Wolf River, was laid out in 1819 by General Andrew Jackson, Judge John

Overton, and General James Winchester on a 5000-acre land grant at the top of the Chickasaw bluffs. Settlement was slowed by recurring epidemics of yellow fever, smallpox, malaria and cholera. The site of the city was well located as a port for both the south and the west, however, and settlement was steady. In 1840, the population of Memphis was 1,799 people. Twenty years later, it topped 18,000.

WHAT TO SEE AND DO IN MEMPHIS

Beale Street Historic District ⚑

The standard advice for anyone visiting Memphis is, "You can't miss Beale Street, Home of the Blues." So we went dutifully to **B. B. King's** on Beale & 2nd Streets and found good-natured crowds, tasty soul food, emotional saxes, and free and easy dancers—indeed a memorable visit. Nightclubs and specialty shops are open year-round.

Mud Island (Parking ❶)

You may find getting to Mud Island confusing. Exit onto Poplar Street for parking. The terminal for the monorail to the island is on Front Street between Adams and Poplar, 901-576-7230. Open April through October. The island's attractions include a scale model of the lower Mississippi, the Mississippi River Museum, and the Memphis Belle. *You'll also find numerous gift shops and eateries here.*

Mud Island, a large park operated by the City of Memphis, is located on an island offshore of the city. It is perhaps best known for a riverwalk which is a scale model of the channels and islands of the lower Mississippi. The **Mississippi River Museum ❷** is also outstanding, with entertaining and insightful displays interpreting settlement, Civil War, slavery, ethnic music and more. An overview of the Museum's 18 galleries starts on page 212.

The Mud Island ticket also includes admittance to a display of the ***Memphis Belle ❸***, the first B-17 bomber to complete 25 missions in World War II. The *Belle* has been featured in several movies.

W. C. Handy Museum and Gallery ④   ⌐

352 Beale Street, 901-527-2583. Open May through September, Tuesday through Saturday, from 10 a.m. to 5 p.m. Sunday, 1 to 5 p.m. Admission fee.

This is the actual home of W. C. Handy, who popularized Beale Street in the 1920s and 30s with his Beale Street Blues. Of interest are historic photos of Beale Street by Ernest Withers.

The Pyramid ⑤

One Auction Avenue, 901-521-1830. Open daily. Admission fee.

The Pyramid is a distinctively shaped sports and entertainment complex. At 32 stories, it's the third tallest pyramid in the world. Its base is the size of six football fields.

Allow plenty of time for your visit to Mud Island and plan to walk this riverwalk, which is a scale model of the winding path of the lower Mississippi.

A Brief Tour of the
Mississippi River Museum at Mud Island

Work on the Mississippi River Museum at Mud Island began in 1977 and was completed in 1982 at a cost of $63 million. There are 18 galleries in the museum, considered to be one of the finest along the river.

1st Gallery: Early Explorers. Artifacts and displays of early European explorers and expeditions, the more permanent forts, and the personal lives of settlers.

2nd Gallery: Steamboat. Replica of an 1870 packet steamboat. Walk around its slanted deck among cotton bales, liquor and molasses kegs, wooden boxes and canvas sacks of sugar, flour and beans. Not only were the steam boilers highly dangerous, shooting sparks all about, but the cargo itself—alcohol, cotton bales, wooden boxes and kegs—was extremely flammable. The boiler is open to view on the first deck—boilers needed to sit on the first deck (rather than below decks) so that the draft of the boat could be just 4 feet or so.

3rd Gallery: Models showing the transition from steam to diesel power.

4th Gallery: Pilot House. A very realistic mock-up of the pilot house of a modern towboat. A modern tow on the lower river can push an unlimited number of barges (15 is the limit on the upper river); 72 is the record on the lower river.

A tow pushes more than 40 barges.

5th Gallery: River People. Portrays the life of those who worked along the river: gamblers, light keepers (yes, while river lights today are electric, men once tended kerosene lamps), levee workers, keelboat men, steamboat captains, pilots and showboat performers.

6th Gallery: River Technology. Demonstrations of the technology of river management. Note especially the willow "mattresses" which for many years served as do concrete mattresses today—to try to maintain the river in its channel and protect unstable mud banks from erosion. Woven willow branches were used because they took root when laid in the mud, and soon the bank was anchored in willow trees. A willow mattress, however, was only effective for about 30 years.

Today Mud Island is completely surrounded by concrete mattresses; in fact, a mattress lies under the cobblestone walkways. Such fortification is not necessary on the upper Mississippi because there the channel is carved in rock, not silt, as it is on the lower river.

Memphis was the site of the first railroad bridge built across the lower Mississippi. Because it took years for engineers to develop a technology for building bridges on deep silt beds, it wasn't built until 1892, long after the Eads Bridge in St. Louis.

Gallery 7: Theatre of Disasters. An 11-minute film portrays river-related disasters—from the New Madrid earthquake to steamboat explosions and a yellow fever epidemic in Memphis.

A concrete "mattress," produced by the Army Corps of Engineers, can be composed of as many as 50,000 rectangles of concrete slabs, each 4 by 25 feet.

Galleries 8 through 12: The Civil War. The galleries provide a very even-handed portrayal of the War.

Gunboats: Note how existing steamboats were modified for war: exterior paddlewheels were boxed in and heavy protection was added to pilot houses. On boats built specifically for war, paddlewheels were placed in the middle of the boat for protection and pilot houses were reduced to narrow windows elevated just off the deck.

Civil war gunboats, possibly at Island #10.

Island # 10 Battle (Island #10 is located near New Madrid, Missouri, and Tiptonville, Tennessee): In order to control the Mississippi, Union forces had to wrest control of Island #10 from the Confederates. The island was so heavily armed that Federal gunboats could not get by at all until two metal gunboats managed to run the gauntlet. Northern forces were able to surround the island and force a Confederate surrender.

The Battle at Memphis involved a boat no one had ever seen before—it had a battering ram at the front. When the eight boats in the Confederate army met the Union boats at Memphis, seven Confederate boats were sunk or captured within 90 minutes. The eighth boat—the last riverboat in the Confederate navy—escaped to Vicksburg, Mississippi. The citizens of Memphis watched the river battle from the bluffs, and when it was over they went to the courthouse and raised an American flag. The Battle of Memphis was over. Today, visitors can view the river from one of those same bluffs from the park at the foot of Union Avenue at Riverside Drive.

The Battle of Vicksburg As you enter this last Civil War gallery, you'll find yourself in the belly of an ironclad gunboat complete with the sounds of raging battle. On exiting the gunboat, you're on the sandbagged bluffs of Vicksburg, looking down on a Union gunboat as the sound of cannon-fire booms all around. It's an experience not to be missed!

Vicksburg was one of the last river ports to fall in the battle for control of the river (the battle below New Orleans was fought with ocean-going vessels). Vicksburg is built on a bluff, like Memphis is, but after the Battle of Memphis, when only one boat remained to the Confederate forces, Confederate officers decided to fight this battle from the bluffs, firing on Federal gunboats trying to pass down the river.

The gunboats could do little to harm the forces dug into the bluffs, so Grant simply bypassed them on land (now the Vicksburg Military Park) and cut a canal from above Vicksburg to the riverbend below the city. Thus Vicksburg was surrounded by troops on land to the east and by northern boats on the river to the north and the south. Grant was able to supply his troops and boats via the canal that bypassed Vicksburg's riverfront.

The siege of Vicksburg lasted for 47 days, with citizens resorting to eating rats, dogs, horses, cats, shoe leather and anything else they could scavenge. They offered to surrender two days before the battle finally ended, but Grant refused to accept until the fourth of July. Thereafter, the 4th was not celebrated in Vicksburg until recent times.

The canal cut by Grant quickly became the main channel of the river, and the city of Vicksburg was left on a "meander spur." The river was finally restored to Vicksburg by the Army Corps of Engineers in the early 1900s so that the city would once again have a port.

Galleries 13 through 17: Multimedia music galleries.

Much of our modern popular music grew out of African music sung by the slaves in the southern fields. As blacks were introduced to Christianity, the words and themes changed and the songs became *spirituals* which are still very popular today. *Gospel music* is an offshoot of the spirituals.

According to the displays, the *blues* came out of work songs and field hollers used not only to pass time in the fields, but to pass along messages. After the slaves were freed and dispersed across the United States, they continued to sing their sad, soulful songs in honkytonks—little bars— mostly for their own entertainment. After the 1900s, as blacks dispersed into the largest cities—Chicago, St. Louis, Harlem—urban blues became popular nationwide. The blues were recorded and published as sheet music.

Ragtime (made popular by Scott Joplin) was developing at about the same time as the blues, but was happy, upbeat music that was fun to listen to. *Barrelhouse blues* resembles rock & roll, and *country blues* resembles modern country music. Much of today's popular music has direct ties with the old slave "blues." *Delta blues* came out of the deep south while *jazz* was born in New Orleans and includes bits of the French and Caribbean music tradition. Radio stations in the south specialize in "old blues" or "new blues." B.B. King recorded well into the 1960s, so there is still plenty of good blues around.

W.C. Handy was the first to publish the blues and thus he has the title "Father of the Blues." The first song he published was the "Memphis Blues," so Memphis became the "Home of the Blues."

Sam Phillips of Memphis owned Sun Studios and was actively trying to develop this blues sound in a white performer for the mass market. When he heard the tape of a young man who had come in to record a song for his mother, he said, "That's it, that's the sound I've been looking for! A white guy that sounds like a black guy."

The young man was Elvis Presley. Sam Phillips went on to record such performers as Chuck Berry, Johnnie Cash, Carl Perkins, and Jerry Lee Lewis.

Gallery 18: River Room: From the windows in this gallery visitors can look over to the opposite shore and directly down at the Mississippi.

The last gallery presents the natural history (flora and fauna) of the Mississippi River Valley and includes a large fresh water aquarium and a live reptile display.

National Civil Rights Museum ❻ ╆

406 Mulberry Street, 901-521-9699. Open Monday through Sunday. Closed Tuesday. Admission fee.

The museum is located at the Lorraine Motel, site of the 1968 assassination of Dr. Martin Luther King, Jr. It is the first museum of its kind in the country, with interpretive exhibits that bring to life the sights, sounds, and tensions of the civil rights movement.

Victorian Village Historic District ❼

From the 1830s to the 1870s, Adams Avenue was the most fashionable address in Memphis. Today, tours of the elegant mansions include the 1836 **Magevny House**, the oldest remaining house in Memphis.

Memphis Queen Line Riverboats ❽

At the foot of Monroe Street at Riverside Drive, 901-527-5694. Sightseeing cruises of all types and times of day from March through November.

Memphis Zoo ❾

2000 Galloway Avenue, 901-276-9453.

This modern metropolitan zoo is home to 2,800 animals of 400 different species. It's considered to have one of the finest wild cat displays in the world.

Graceland

3734 Elvis Presley Blvd., 800-237-2000. The Platinum Tour is about $20 and includes guided tours of Graceland, its grounds, Elvis's airplane, and various Presley collections. It's easy to spend several hours there touring or visiting restaurants and gift shops.

Our visit to Graceland, the Memphis estate of Elvis Presley, left us convinced that the world had indeed lost a dedicated performer when Elvis died in 1977 at age 42. He made 33 movies and sold more records than any other individual performer in American history.

The continued dedication of his fans was notable. A woman in line turned to me mournfully and confided, "I had a ticket to see his last performance."

"Was it good?" I asked.

"I never got to see it," she sighed. "I couldn't get anyone at work to cover for me so I could go." The sadness in her voice and demeanor were palpable.

"He was so good," she continued. "He was such a great musician and performer; he worked so hard for his fans. That's what he cared about most—doing what his fans needed to have a good time."

Tour Elvis's plane, the Lisa Marie, *at Graceland.*

South Memphis

Chucalissa Archaeological Museum

1987 Indian Village Drive, 901-785-3160.

While due for a facelift, Chucalissa is a good place to visit if you're interested in the Mississippian mound culture. Walk through a cross-section of an archeological excavation in which postholes, foundation posts, and old campfires are identified. Exit the cut into a thatched cottage with an elaborate diorama set up inside. The reconstructed 15th century Mississippian Indian village was developed in the 1930s to show how it would have looked with thatched houses and mounds.

Each of the Mississippian mound sites along the river is slightly different, and by visiting all of them—Cahokia Mounds near St. Louis, Wickliffe, Chucalissa, and nearby Parkin Archeological Site in Arkansas—visitors can become quite knowledgeable about the Mississippian culture. See Appendix A for a time line of prehistoric settlement.

T. O. Fuller State Park   ▲ ⚶

1500 Mitchell Road West, Memphis, 901-543-7581. Next to Chucalissa, southwest of U.S. Highway 61 and I-55, 11 miles southwest of downtown Memphis. Camping, 18-hole golf course, picnicking, and swimming pool.

This is a 384-acre green oasis on the outskirts of the city.

─────────── ☼ ───────────

The route continues across the river into Arkansas on I-40. Turn north on I-55 and continue to Hwy. 64 at Marion, Arkansas, just north of West Memphis to visit the Parkin Archeological Site on Hwy. 64 at Marion, Arkansas, just north of West Memphis. From Memphis, it's 7 miles to West Memphis, AR, and 133 miles to Little Rock.

Thatched granary and stockade wall at Chucalissa.

Appendices

Trapper Falls Cabin

CREDITS

Front cover photo © Basil Williams

Back cover photo © David Haggard

p. 4, St. Louis photo, Rich Middleton

p. 9, Cahokia Mounds photo, Mike Coles

p. 18, Clovis Points photo, Illinois State Museum

p. 19, mastodon, Mastodon State Historic Site, Missouri DNR

p. 24, Barbagallo house photo, Kimmswick Historical Society

p. 66, longlots map, National Archives, Washington, DC

p. 34, photo, courtesy Church of the Holy Family

p. 37, photos, Cahokia Courthouse State Historic Site

p. 52, painting, Charles H. Wallis, courtesy of the Corner George B&B

p. 81, map of Fort, Fort de Chartres State Historic Site

p. 82, photo, Jim DuVall

p. 86, drawing of Menard, Pierre Menard Home State Historic Site

p. 129, painting, Cairo Custom House Museum

p. 178, mounds drawing, *History of Illinois, 1884*

p. 185, flood mural, City of Paducah

p. 200, photo, Tennessee Tourism Development Office

p. 202, bowfin drawing, Maynard F. Reece, Iowa DNR

p. 153, Bollinger Mill photo, Nick Decker, Missouri DNR

p. 161, New Madrid Observation Deck photo, New Madrid Chamber of Commerce

p. 166, Hunter Dawson Home photo, Missouri DNR

p. 172, Towosahgy sketch, Missouri DNR

p. 195, photo, Rich Middleton

p. 224, Prehistoric Settlement Timeline—Chucalissa Archaeological Museum

Photos are by Pat Middleton unless otherwise credited.

BOOKLIST

Complete History of Illinois, 1663-1884, H.W. Rokker, Springfield, IL, publishers

Comprehensive Plan for the Illinois Nature Preserves, John E. Schwegman, principal author

The French Colony in the Mid-Mississippi Valley by Margaret Brown and Lawrie Cena Dean, American Kestrel Books, Carbondale, IL

From Arrowheads to Aerojets: History of Monroe County, 1673-1966, Ed. Helen R. Kline, Myron Roever Assoc.

A Guide to the Geology of the Columbia and Waterloo Area—Field Trip Guide Book, April 1997, Department of Natural Resources, Illinois, State Geological Survey

Historic Names and Places on the Lower Mississippi River, U.S. Army Corps of Engineers

The Mighty Mississippi by Lori Erickson, The Globe Pequote Press, Old Saybrook, CT

Missouri: A History by Paul Nagel

Personal Memoirs of Ulysses S. Grant, published by Charles L. Webster & Co., 1885

Reelfoot Lake and the New Madrid Fault, Juanita Clifton/Lou Harshaw, Victor Publishing Co., Ashville, NC

The Sac and Fox, by Bonvilain, Chelsea House, New York

The Story of Old Ste. Genevieve by Gregory M. Franzwa, The Patrice Press, St. Louis, MO

Tennessee's Indian Peoples, Ronald N. Satz, University of Tennessee Press, Knoxville, TN

The Time of the French in the Heart of North America by Charles J. Balesi, Alliance Français, Chicago

A Brief History of the
Lower Mississippi River

PREHISTORIC SETTLEMENT
Source: Chucalissa Archaeological Museum, Memphis

20,000 BC to 8,000 BC: Paleo-Indians These very earliest humans lived in natural shelters and hunted mastodons. (Visit the mastodon site outside Ste. Genevieve, Missouri.)

8000 BC to 1500 BC: Archaic-Indians Hunters and gatherers who learned to grind grain and to weave. (Visit the Modoc Shelter, Modoc, Illinois.)

1500 BC to 900 BC : Woodland Indians They learned pottery-making in the late Archaic times and developed agriculture in the Woodland period, cultivating squash, beans and corn. They also developed the bow and arrow during this period. Earthen mounds are characteristic of this era.

900 AD to 1500 AD: Mississippian Period This was the most advanced culture known to exist in the Southeast. They reached their peak between 1200 and 1500 AD. Their religion was based on sun worship, and they had a unique art style in tools, ornaments and pottery. Their most distinctive cultural trait was building large earthen mounds (platform mounds) as foundations for temples, council houses, and dwellings for tribal leaders. They raised corn, beans, and squash and lived in villages, some as large as 10,000-20,000 people.

UNDER SPANISH RULE

1541 De Soto is the first European to explore southern reaches of the Mississippi. He may have had contact with Choctaw or Chickasaw Indians in Mississippi.

1764 While Spain controls Missouri, few immigrants are Spanish. Daniel Boone arrives in 1798 to a grant of 8,500 acres (west of St. Louis). Others from Kentucky and Tennessee are recruited.

UNDER FRENCH RULE
Source: A Kaskaskia Chronology *by Herb Meyer*

1605- 1670 France begins to colonize North America. By 1666, the population of New France (Canada) is more than 3,400.

1673 Marquette and Joliet record their travels on the Mississippi River as far southward as the mouth of the Arkansas River and back up the Illinois River. A few French traders become established and European goods are increasingly available to the natives by 1674.

1690-1700 The Tamaroa and Cahokia bands of the Illini establish villages in the vicinity of present-day Cahokia. Father de St. Cosme establishes a mission here in 1699.

1703 Bands of peaceable Kaskaskia and Tamaroa settle on the Kaskaskia River "two leagues upstream from the Mississippi River." The mission of Kaskaskia is established by Father Marest.

1717-1722 Civil government by the French is established for the new province of Illinois. Previously the area was considered part of Canada; it now becomes officially a part of the Louisiana Colony.

1720 The first Fort de Chartres is completed. It is small, made of posts or palisades in a square plan. Soon after, St. Anne (the Prairie of Fort de Chartres) originates close by. The Village of Kaskaskia is described as having about 80 houses and a new stone church to replace the original church of vertical log posts.

1722 Prairie du Rocher is established. In 1725 a second Fort de Chartres is built.

1735 Old Ste. Genevieve is established on the west bank of the Mississippi. Kaskaskia is said to have a population of 388 whites.

1747 The French garrison moves to Kaskaskia.

1756 Fort de Chartres is rebuilt of stone at enormous expense to the French.

1763 The French and Indian War ends. The Treaty of Paris cedes all land east of the Mississippi to England. In November, Laclède arrives at Fort de Chartres and spends the winter.

1764 Laclède begins his trading post opposite Cahokia and by 1765 fifty families have moved to San Carlos, the future city of St. Louis. Meanwhile, other families are moving west to Ste. Genevieve.

1769 Pontiac is murdered in Cahokia.

1778 George Rogers Clark occupies British Kaskaskia and Cahokia without serious incident in July. In February of 1779 his small army forces the surrender of Vincennes and ends British dominance in the Illinois Country.

THE AMERICAN PERIOD

1792 Kentucky admitted as the 15th state. It is the first state west of the Appalachians to join the Union.

1784-1796 After the American Revolution, the inhabitants of Tennessee form an independent government, the state of *Franklin*. Tennessee is eventually admitted as the 16th state in 1796.

1785-1787 A major flood causes the abandonment of Old Ste. Genevieve and causes extensive damage in Kaskaskia. In 1787, Illinois becomes part of the new Northwest Territory under the American government. Slavery is forbidden north of the Ohio River.

1803 Napoleon offers President Thomas Jefferson the vast reaches along the Mississippi and Missouri rivers (Louisiana Territory) for $15 million.

1804 The Lewis and Clark expedition strengthens U.S. claims from St. Louis to the Pacific. The Kaskaskia Indians cede their land claims to the U.S. government and a tide of white settlement is under way.

1811-1812 The earthquakes centered in New Madrid, Missouri, ring church bells as far away as Boston. The little steamboat *New Orleans* finds itself adrift in the raging rivers of the Mississippi. The War of 1812 coincides with increased "Indian troubles" in Illinois.

1818 Illinois becomes the 21st state, and Kaskaskia is named its capital. In 1820 the state capital is moved to Vandalia and Kaskaskia's decline begins.

1820 The Missouri Compromise allows Missouri admittance to the Union as a slave state, though the boundary line would henceforth be the southern boundary of Missouri. This was to counterbalance Main, which became a free state at the same time.

1821 President James Monroe names Missouri as the 24th state. Stephen Austin leaves with 300 Missourians to settle his Texas land grant.

1823 *Virginia* steams all the way to Fort Snelling in Minnesota. By the 1850s, St. Louis received more than 3,000 steamboats and a million tons of freight per year. In 1989, barges carrying more than 8 million tons passed through the lock at Alton, Illinois.

1838 By this time, the native Choctaw, Cherokee and Chickasaw Indians of Tennessee and Mississippi were forcibly removed west of the Mississippi to reservations in Oklahoma.

1839 The Mormons are brutally driven from Missouri. Bloody conflicts consume the western part of the state over the future of slavery between Kansas and Missouri. Bitter vengeance became standard through the Civil War and for twenty years after the end of the war. This period of lawlessness culminated in the death of Jesse James in the 1880s.

1861 Invention of the telegraph puts an end to the year-long saga of the Pony Express out of St. Joseph, Missouri. Brigham Young sends the first telegram: *Utah stands firm with the Union.* Tennessee and Missouri suffer through more battles and skirmishes than any other state but Virginia during the Civil War.

1863-1905 The Mississippi River begins a shift to the east at a place just south of Ste. Genevieve. By 1879 a large bend has formed which brings the river to within a half mile of the Kaskaskia River about six miles above its mouth. The Mississippi begins to undermine many acres of land until in April of 1881 it breaks through and flows in a great torrent down the Kaskaskia River. Until 1905, the river munches away at the town, its streets, and its buildings until there is hardly any trace of the village and its two centuries of inhabitants.

1865 The *Sultana* sinks with 2000 Union soldiers returning home from southern prison camps.

1874 Eads Bridge (the "impossible" bridge) spans the Mississippi River at St. Louis. Engineer James Eads (American Hall of Fame) also built the ironclad boats that permitted the Union to claim the Mississippi River during the Civil War.

1904 World's Fair held in St. Louis commemorates centennial of Lewis and Clark expedition.

1925 Tennessee attracts international attention with the *Scopes Trial,* which tested a state law forbidding the teaching of evolution.

1927 Charles Lindbergh flies the *Spirit of St. Louis* from New York to Paris in the first non-stop transatlantic flight.

A Guide to River Miles, Cairo to Memphis

River miles for the Upper River are counted from Mile 0.0 at Cairo, Illinois to Mile 839.0 at Lambert Landing in St. Paul, Minnesota. River miles for the Lower Mississippi are counted from 0.0 at Head of Passes (AHP), 90 miles below New Orleans, Louisiana, and increase to Mile 953.8 near Cairo at the confluence of the Ohio River. By air, the distance between the Ohio River confluence and Head of Passes is only 600 miles! A listing of river miles for major landmarks and towns along the Lower River follows. Right/Left bank designations apply to boats *descending* the river.

179.5 (Upper River) St. Louis, MO. Laclède Levee. Jefferson National Expansion Memorial riverfront park. Gateway Arch, Lewis & Clark Museum in St. Charles, Old Cathedral, Old Courthouse.

953.8 Cairo, IL. Fort Defiance and confluence of the Ohio River.

937.2 *left* Columbus-Belmont State Park, Columbus, Illinois.

936.8 *right* Belmont, Missouri.

933.0 *right* Wolf Island, KY. Once a large 15,000 acre island. In 1820, John James Audubon noted large numbers of ivory-billed woodpeckers.

923.0 *right* Barge terminal and grain elevator in Dorena area, Missouri.

922.0 *left* Hickman, KY. Car ferry to Dorena.

914.0 *right* Island #8, one of the largest existing islands. Now silting in on the right bank.

901.0 *right* Island #10, originally a small island close to Tennessee, now incorporated into the Missouri shore.

888.0 *right* New Madrid, MO.

873.0 *left* Tiptonville, TN, now located nearly a mile inland of the river. Reelfoot Lake is several miles inland of Tiptonville.

846.0 *right* Caruthersville, MO.

819.2 *left* Obion River enters the Mississippi. Indian for "many pronged." Legend suggests that Davy Crockett killed 105 bears near the mouth of the Obion.

779.5 *left* Fort Pillow, TN. Civil War battlefield.

778.0 *left* Fulton, TN.

774.0 *left* Hatchie River, abundant wildlife and waterfowl.

743.4 *right* Redman Point, AK. It was near here, during a night in December 1865, that the steamboat *Sultana* exploded her boilers and sank with 2000 Union soldiers returning from southern prison camps. Most drowned in the cold, swift current.

735.0 *left* Memphis, TN.

APPENDIX C
State, Regional and Local Tourism Contacts

STATE

Illinois
Tourism Information
100 W. Randolph St.
Ste. 3-400
Chicago, IL 60601
1-800-226-6632
Fax 217-785-6554
http://www.enjoyillinois.com

Kentucky
Kentucky Tourism Cabinet
Capital Plaza Tower, 24th Floor
Frankfort, KY 40601
502-564-4270
Fax 502-564-6100

Tourism
800-225-TRIP, ext 67
Fax 615-741-7225

State Park Information
800-255-PARK

Missouri
Missouri Division of Tourism
P.O. Box 1055
Jefferson City, MO 65102
314-751-4133

*Missouri Department
of Natural Resources*
800-334-6946

Tennessee
Tennessee Dept. of Tourism
P.O. Box 23170
Nashville, TN 37202
615-741-2159

Arkansas
*Arkansas Department of Parks
and Tourism*
One Capitol Mall
Little Rock, AK 72201
501-682-1120
Fax 501-682-1364

REGIONAL

*Southernmost Illinois
Tourism Bureau*
P.O. Box 278, Exit 18 off I-57
Ullin, IL 62992
800-248-4373
E-mail: sitc@intrnet.net
http://www.intrnet.net/~sitc/

Southwestern Illinois CVB
10950 Lincoln Trail
Fairview Heights, IL 62208
800-442-1488
Email: info@illinoissouthwest.org
www.illinoissouthwest.org

NW Tennessee Tourism
(Reelfoot Lake)
901-587-4215

Shawnee National Forest
800-406-6418

LOCAL

Illinois

Greater Alton/
Twin Rivers CVB
200 Piasa
Alton, IL 62002
800-ALTON-IL

Cache River Wetlands
Illinois DNR
930 Sunflower Lane
Belknap, IL 62908
618-634-9678

Cairo Chamber of Commerce
Cairo, IL 62914
618-734-2737

Carbondale, IL
800-526-1500

Collinsville CVB
(Cahokia Mounds)
1 Gateway Drive (Off I-55)
Collinsville, IL 62234
800-289-2388

Cypress Creek National
Wildlife Area
618-634-2231

Maeystown, 62256
618-458-6660

Olive Branch Chamber
of Commerce
Olive Branch, IL 62969
618-776-5541

Prairie du Rocher, IL 62277
618-284-3463

Randolph County Tourism P.O.
Box 332
Chester, IL 62233
618-826-5000, ext. 221
http://www.egyptian.net/~rndlfedc

Trail of Tears State Forest
618-833-4910

Waterloo Winery
725 N. Market Street
Waterloo, IL 62298

Missouri

Cape Girardeau CVB
P.O. Box 617, 2121 Broadway
Cape Girardeau, MO 63702-0617
800-777-0068 or 573-335-1631

Caruthersville
573-333-1222

Charleston
573-683-3325

East Prairie
573-649-3425
Fax 573-649-2452

Kimmswick Historical
Society
314-464-TOUR

Mastodon State Historic Site
Imperioal, MO 63052
314-464-2976

City of New Madrid
Department of Tourism
P.O. Box 96
New Madrid, MO 63869
573-748-2866
Fax 573-748-5402

Sikeston
Chamber of Commerce
573-471-2498

St. Charles CVB
230 S. Main
St. Charles, MO 63301
800-366-2427
Email:gsccvb@ix.netcom.com
Internet: www.st-charles.mo.us

Ste. Genevieve
800-373-7007

St. Louis
800-916-0040
Email:webmaster@st-louis-cvc.com
www.st.louis-cvc.com

Trail of Tears State Park
(near Cape Girardeau)
573-334-1711

230

Kentucky

Columbus-Belmont State Park
502-677-2327

Hickman
502-326-2902

*Paducah-McCracken
County CVB*
128 Broadway
Paducah, KY 42001
800-359-4775
E-mail: fun@paducah-tourism.org
www.paducah-tourism.org

Wickliffe Mounds
Murray State University
Research Center
Wickliffe, KY
502-335-3681

Tennessee

Fort Pillow State Historic Area
Rte 2, Box 108 B-1
Henning, TN
901-738-5581

Memphis CVB
47 Union Avenue
Memphis, TN 38103
901-543-5300
800-8-MEMPHIS
http://www.memphistravel.com

Reelfoot Lake State Park
Tiptonville, TN 38079
901-253-7756

Reelfoot Lake Tourism Office
PO Box 9, Dept. K-V
Samburg, TN 38254
901-538-2666

Mississippi

Vicksburg CVB
PO Box 1100
Vicksburg, MS 39181
800-221-3536

Index

A reinforced levee protects Ste. Genevieve, Missouri in 1993.

About the Author

Pat Middleton is a writer, publisher, and lecturer living along the Mississippi River near La Crosse, Wisconsin. Pat is a frequent guest lecturer aboard the great steamboats cruising the Mississippi River and contributes regularly to many midwestern and national magazines.

Pat speaks throughout the Midwest to educators, writers, schoolchildren, historians, travel groups, and radio and television audiences, sharing her enthusiasm about her craft and the great Mississippi River, its heritage and natural history.

Visit Pat's Mississippi River Home Page on the World Wide Web for a wealth of free Mississippi River travel and educational resources at **http://www.greatriver.com**

Ordering Information

If you have enjoyed reading Pat Middleton's guide to the Lower Mississippi River, you will want to order Volumes 1 and 2, the highly acclaimed volumes that complete the series:

Discover!
America's Great River Road
Volume 1: St. Paul to Dubuque
$13.95

Discover!
America's Great River Road
Volume 2: Dubuque to St. Louis
$13.95

For children grades 3 to 5, order

Mississippi River Activity Guide for Kids, $5.50

Teacher Resource Kits , $24 to $63

Call direct **(608-457-2734)** to charge your order or send your personal check or money order to the following address. (Include $3.50 shipping for the first book plus $1.50 for each additional book; Wisconsin residents, please add 5.5% sales tax.)

Heritage Press
W987 Cedar Valley Road
Stoddard, WI 54658

You may also order books in the **Discover!** series online at our Mississippi River "supersite," **The Mississippi River Home Page**. River buffs will enjoy browsing our *Insight* features on such topics as commercial fish markets and treasure hunting along the river:

http://www.greatriver.com
E-mail: Heritage@greatriver.com